thrive

*Matt —
Go forth and
thrive!
Blaine Stockler*

thrive

TEN PRESCRIPTIONS FOR
EXCEPTIONAL PERFORMANCE
AS A COMMERCIAL REAL ESTATE AGENT

BLAINE STRICKLAND

Copyrighted Material

Thrive: Ten Prescriptions for Exceptional Performance as a Commercial Real Estate Agent

Copyright © 2018 by Resourceful Publishing, LLC. All Rights Reserved.

No part of this publication may be reproduced, stored in a retrieval system or transmitted, in any form or by any means—electronic, mechanical, photocopying, recording or otherwise—without prior written permission from the publisher, except for the inclusion of brief quotations in a review.

For information about this title or to order other books and/or electronic media, contact the publisher:

Resourceful Publishing, LLC
8604 Mindich Court, Orlando, FL 32819
www.hbs-resources.com
blaine@hbs-resources.com

Library of Congress Control Number:

Print: 978-0-9997690-0-3
eBook: 978-0-9997690-1-0
Audio: 978-0-9997690-2-7

Printed in the United States of America

Cover and Interior design: 1106 Design

CONTENTS

PREFACE xi

FOREWORD *by Rod Santomassimo* xiii

INTRODUCTION xvii

PART ONE:
BECOME A DOMINANT FORCE

CHAPTER 1: Prospecting isn't fun, and I'm already too busy
Prescription: Use a simple, top-of-mind system to maximize your prospecting 1

CHAPTER 2: I have more projects than I can manage
Prescription: Use the tool that professional project managers use—a Gantt chart 9

CHAPTER 3: Too much time gets wasted on deals that fall apart in the end
Prescription: Employ a masterful due-diligence process as if you were a principal 17

CHAPTER 4: I should be much more dominant in my niche

> *Prescription: Invoke your "power to convene" to become the undisputed leader* **25**

PART TWO:

BUILD A TEAM

CHAPTER 5: Why am I working on these administrative tasks? I need help!

> *Prescription: Use this proven process to find and employ an effective assistant* **33**

CHAPTER 6: I have an assistant, but it is not working (again)

> *Prescription: Turn your assistant into an accelerator for your business* **41**

CHAPTER 7: We make the same mistakes over and over again

> *Prescription: Take time to carefully refine your goals and create revealing metrics* **47**

CHAPTER 8: I know he drags our team down, but I just can't let him go

> *Prescription: The wrong player in the wrong seat must be remedied* **55**

PART THREE:

RUN YOUR OPERATION AS A BUSINESS

CHAPTER 9: I hate this time of year—I dread always having to start over

Prescription: A business like yours demands a cash-flow projection 63

CHAPTER 10: My broker cares only about the next check I am supposed to bring in

Prescription: Derive maximum value from your brokerage platform 69

CONCLUSION 75

APPENDIX

A. A word to managing brokers (or owners) of a commercial real estate brokerage 83

B. A detailed pipeline system 87

C. Books that have been meaningful to me 91

ACKNOWLEDGMENTS 97

ABOUT THE AUTHOR 99

This book is the fulfillment of a promise I made to Mrs. Margaret Fortier a long time ago. As my fourth-grade teacher in Anchorage, Alaska, she was a tough task mistress but a loving inspiration, too. After I turned in my report on the Alaskan flag, Eight Stars of Gold on a Field of Blue (crafted, without mistakes, in fountain pen), she told me that I should write a book someday, and I promised I would. We communicated for many years, and I cried when I received the inevitable letter from her husband. I've looked at the Big Dipper thousands of times in the night sky since then. Each time, it reminds me of the Alaska state flag and my promise to Mrs. Fortier. Even though I can't put my book in her hands, I am so pleased to have finally delivered.

PREFACE

The economic downturn caused by the Great Recession crushed me. By the end of 2011, all of the properties and all of my teammates were gone. I took the last chair and the last computer from my corporate office and moved into my house. I really had no choice other than to start working out of my house and call myself a consultant. Because I had a couple of teaching gigs lined up, I knew I wouldn't make $0 in 2012, but my outlook wasn't exactly positive, either.

I decided not to panic. I had been through cycles before, and I knew that recovery would eventually come. I also knew that I had accumulated years of experience and honed certain skills that could be valuable to other people. Slowly, opportunities arose to work with agents, brokers, and companies that were also trying to recover. Assignments began to roll in, deals began to transact, and commissions began to flow again.

Within just a few years, many of these agents began to have their best years—even better than the peaks of the pre-Recession years. With that success, many agents struggled with the problems of success: too many assignments, not enough structure, too many broken promises. Agents turned to me to help them try to resolve the basic problem: Their ability to develop the business far exceeded their ability to execute it. This was a common situation, and I had many opportunities to work with agents and teams that were desperate to create a sustainable business model.

The prescriptions in this book are the result of long hours working with agents at all tiers of the business as they sought to gain control of and enhance their performance.

This book is for agents who are already making money as commissioned salespeople. I assume you have already experienced some success and pain. My hope is that I can help you mitigate the pain and accelerate the success. I want this book to be *inspirational* for you, helping you see a way to improve your performance so you are inspired to make the changes required to achieve greater success.

I would be pleased to learn that agents newer to the business also read and learn from this book. My hope for you is that the message of the book is *aspirational,* helping you aspire to be very successful, particularly as you learn from us "old dogs." You may well find that you recognize these issues on your current team or even on the horizon of your own practice. In that case, read this book now and pass it around—but read it again in two years.

Finally, let's be clear about *broker* and *agent.* It is common parlance in the industry to refer to all of the commissioned salespeople in a commercial real estate brokerage company as "brokers." Using common licensing law terminology, some of these people may hold broker licenses, while others hold salesperson licenses. To further confuse the lingo, many commissioned salespeople will refer to their licensed manager as "my broker." Simultaneously, the manager may refer to the sales team as "my agents." To be as clear as possible in this book, I've used *agent* when referring to the person (you?) who is focused on earning commissions. I've used *broker* when referring to the person who owns or runs the brokerage company.

FOREWORD

I remember that day in 2012 like it was yesterday. I met Blaine for an early morning breakfast, before he flew back from his adjunct teaching role at the University of North Carolina to his home in Orlando, Florida. Blaine shared with me his thoughts about working as one of my coaches at the Massimo Group. "Rod—I have good news and bad news for you. The good news is that you have something here. The bad news is that you're doing it all wrong."

I simply stared at him in partial disbelief. My first commercial real estate brokerage book had just hit #1 on Amazon. My idea of building a commercial real estate coaching company, four years earlier, had evolved from working by myself at my dining room table to now having five coaches, including Blaine, learning my methodologies and implementing them to over a hundred clients. *Really*, I thought. *Can't he see how successful I've become?*

That's when I made one of the most impactful decisions of my business's growth. I could either pound on my chest and ignore Blaine, or I could ask him what he meant by my "doing it all wrong." Fortunately, I chose the latter.

Blaine was right. I was running a coaching business as a coach, not as an owner. Our client growth was spotty, so our coaches had to call prospects to build our client base. Once we landed a client, there was less structure than I dared to admit, and the client experience was inconsistent. Additionally, I was coaching twenty-five people myself, and was crazy busy. As far as a personal life, forget it; I had none. My wife and two children simply tolerated the long hours I was putting in.

Fortunately, I looked at Blaine and proposed that he help me fix what was broken in my organization. I asked him to not only continue our relationship as one of the Massimo Group's commercial real estate coaches, but also expand his role to become my personal business coach. Before Blaine headed to the airport that morning, we agreed that he would assist me in addressing challenges within the Massimo Group and to create an infrastructure for exponential growth.

Today, with Blaine's personal guidance and my orchestration, the Massimo Group consists of twenty-five commercial real estate coaches and has served over 1,200 clients. We are well-positioned for even greater growth. We have implemented a series of new processes, programs, and support personnel, allowing our coaching clients to achieve exponential results. I spend my time as an owner/leader of a coaching organization, and step outside the whirlwind of everyday management life. Oh, and my wife and kids really like the changes as well.

I first met Blaine in the early 1990s in Tampa, Florida. At that time, he was representing a national developer/landlord and I was representing national insurance companies from a tenant perspective. I was simply starting out. Blaine had already forged his reputation as a shrewd, competent negotiator.

Blaine brings a unique set of skills to the table as a business coach/consultant. He is extremely knowledgeable about the commercial real estate brokerage business. He's been licensed in Florida since 1978, and he collected his first commission in 1979. He graduated with an undergraduate and graduate degree from the University of Florida and earned his CCIM designation in 1987. He was a star for CBRE right out of the box—top producer in his office and then profit center manager. At 29 years of age, he managed an office of 42 people, including agents, mortgage brokers, property managers, and a slew of staffers. Along the way, he's been an appraiser, a developer, a syndicator, a professor, an owner, a property manager, and a consultant. The guy knows his stuff.

Blaine is a voracious consumer of knowledge. He easily reads one book a week. Better yet, he can digest the most valuable lessons from the book and apply them to specific challenges as they arise. One of the first things Blaine asked me to do was read Michael Gerber's *The E-Myth Revisited*, an international best seller. I soon recognized I was just like Sarah the pie-maker. I was acting as a manager, not an owner. I had not implemented the right processes to allow the Massimo Group to grow.

Just as valuable as Blaine's experience and knowledge, though, is his almost extreme desire to define the issues at hand and explore alternative solutions. Blaine is very curious—he intakes a lot of information and uses it to sift through all angles of a challenge, reaching, surprisingly quickly, the heart of the matter. His brain works like a puzzle solver—he sees implications long before most of the rest of us do.

Since that early morning discussion in 2012, I have worked with Blaine on many Massimo Group consulting assignments. We have conducted several engagements working side by side with our clients "locked in the room" with only our notes, a whiteboard, and large self-stick easel pads; *lots* of easel pads. We are usually working toward resolving issues that are muting the client's productivity. These clients are generally owners and/or brokers of individual offices of national CRE organizations, owners of independent firms, or leaders of teams within these organizations.

I usually let Blaine lead the show, which enables me to evaluate all the input and guide the output. The best moments occur after all the easel sheets are hung on the walls, and the clients begin to see the solutions to their challenges develop right in front of their eyes. These are the times I most enjoy working with Blaine. It's as if he is the conductor in a virtual storm of issues, frustrations, opportunities and visions, and he directs all participants from the confusion of the storm to a place of clarity and confidence.

Blaine does for the clients what he has done for me: he has pointed out areas that need improvement and offered proactive solutions. He's not afraid to confront issues, and he stays involved with you after the solutions have been identified. He doesn't get all the credit—and he doesn't claim it; he knows that he simply refocuses the vision, passion, perseverance, and grit of the clients.

That is what has happened at the Massimo Group. My team and I have worked with hundreds of commercial real estate brokers and/or agents either one-on-one or in small teams, including many of the nation's top producers. We are now considered the premier commercial real estate coaching firm and work with clients associated with all of the national firms, as well as many regional and local firms.

With my perspective as a client and a colleague, I'm very pleased to recommend Blaine to you because he has walked in your shoes. He has the experience to help you craft a plan that will navigate you to your desired destination for your organization and/or team.

As you read through his wisdom, I'm confident you'll start to see solutions that apply to your current challenges. As any good doctor would, Blaine has quickly and clearly defined some of the most common pains we find in the commercial real estate business. Blaine then crafts a prescription, which, when filled and taken as directed, will cure what ails you.

Rod N. Santomassimo
Founder/CEO
The Massimo Group, Inc.
August 2017

INTRODUCTION

My perspective on the commercial real estate brokerage business completely changed one day in 1984.

One day I was the top producer in my office of the largest brokerage company in the nation, and the next day I was the sales manager, with the responsibility of managing the sales agents, and coaching them toward their potential. I was now a salaried, non-producing sales manager. How did that happen?

I accepted the offer from the company to leave the sales cube and move into the sales manager role. This meant I would no longer live solely on commissions I generated myself; instead, I would have a boss, a job description, a salary with bonus, a company car, and an office with a door.

I wasn't really attracted by all of those benefits, though. I really wanted to coach. My father and grandfather were professional sports coaches, and I saw the impact they had on their players. I saw a lot of potential in some of the new salespeople around me (my players), and I knew they were in danger of failing. When I was given the opportunity to "hire, train, and retain" producers for the company, I jumped at the chance.

I loved that job, and I worked hard at it. There were many successes, including the transformation of a salesperson who saw himself as a loser grow into a leader in the office. This success caused me to be promoted to profit center manager in a different office. I inherited a lot of salespeople I hadn't hired or trained, and we had to suffer through a failing market. I even had to hire a sales manager to report to me. It was the most challenging role I've ever had, and it forced me to come to grips with a new perspective.

That was over thirty years ago. I realized that salespeople need coaching. Regardless of their personal attributes, background, experiences, trade area, or teammates—commercial real estate salespeople reach maximum success when they have an effective coach by their side. The coach might be a fellow salesperson, a dedicated manager, a mentor, or a specialist in the field. Since then, I have never stopped evolving as a coach. Several economic cycles have come and gone, and because much of my career has been in Florida, I watched those cycles play out at very sharp angles. I have interacted closely with thousands of agents in my role as broker, manager, owner, CCIM instructor, and coach. I've witnessed a lot of successes and failures, including my own.

Today, the commercial real estate brokerage industry faces an unprecedented challenge. Like all businesses in the 21st century, we must assimilate the influence of global markets, dynamic technology, and changing delivery models. We have all of those challenges, plus one more: *enabling a rising agent to envision and launch a compelling career path.*

The National Association of Realtors announced in 2015 that the median age of its commercial members is 60 years of age. Think about that—half the commercial agents in the country are over 60! In the next decade, most of these agents will move out of the industry. The rising agents will be saying goodbye to a generation of agents that endured a complete retooling of the industry and did the best they could to survive during some of the most economically diverse periods in our history. Many have deep, even disabling, battle scars. I've been in many conversations with peers in which they tell me that they advised their children not to follow them into the industry. One claimed that it would be felony child abuse to draw his son into the business to work alongside him.

What, then, is the future for the next generation of agents—*your future*? What legacy are you inheriting? How well are you prepared for your career? How will you even craft a career?

DO YOU RECOGNIZE THIS AGENT?

Like most commercial real estate agents, John started his career working for a third-party brokerage. John didn't get much training.

The plan for John was to shadow a more senior agent. He was told to "work hard, learn your market, and try to find a niche you can master." Fortunately, John started in an upswing market, and deals came together easily.

Now John has managed to survive a downturn and even has two young agents to supervise. He wants to help them so that they cause him to be more effective—and prosperous! John doesn't really know how to help them—he can only use the same training methods and materials to which he was exposed. John can't really explain his approach to the business—somehow, he has just managed to survive.

I call this the "tribal folklore" approach to coaching. You rely on an insufficient program from the past. You don't know how to build a brokerage practice that is durable, sustainable, and moderately predictable. You want to enjoy a blossoming reputation and a consistent stream of income that rolls over and increases from year to year, and even bring others along the journey with you; but you've never been shown how.

Ouch.

Here's the problem: this tribal folklore approach has resulted in sufficiency but not mastery, and it rarely enables someone like you to achieve a career that reaches your potential. You might have changed tribes, seeking a stronger approach or a better fit. But you probably brought your old mentality with you: *I work hard, I track the market, and I try to focus on a specific type of transaction.* Will you ever make the leap from "agent flowing from one transaction to another, seeking to find someone to represent" to "small business owner with a durable client base and a sustainable business plan?"

Your unrealized, perhaps unconscious decision to merely feed off the available transactions usually leads to a fatalistic view of the market and your personal earning capability. You feel, as your predecessors did, that you have to "make hay when the sun is shining" and "hang in there when the market inevitably tanks." Even in the upswing years, you suffer an annual fit of depression as you sense that you have to start over—either because you have to slide back to the bottom of the commission structure in your employment agreement or because you are facing an uncertain market or both.

If you want to break the cycle, it will help to understand how the industry has changed and what it means for you.

HERE'S HOW WE GOT HERE

To fully understand your past and completely retool your future, we have to take a moment to remember how we (you and I and the industry) got to this point.

Four factors have shaped our industry over the past thirty years and are still in effect today:

1. A low barrier to entry has transformed the industry into a disparate cast of characters pursuing a wide range of strategies, most of which are unsuccessful. This means that consistent performers are few and far between.

2. The Resolution Trust Company (RTC) crisis in the late 1980s essentially eliminated non-producing sales managers (those mentors who might have helped us focus on a strategic approach) from the commercial real estate industry. To this day, there are almost no non-producing managers in the industry, which means that salespeople are forced to rely on the tribal lore ("coach yourself") for guidance.

3. Since the recovery from the RTC crisis, many of the agents who have survived, even succeeded, have done it by sheer force of will rather than any disciplined plan. As a result, the role models you've been offered are more brawn than brain. Only a few agents can use this brute-force strategy effectively; this is not a model most people can employ.

4. The independent contractor relationship that has come to dominate the commercial real estate industry has evolved to where it is misunderstood by both agent and broker, but devastatingly, mostly by the agent. As a result, agents rarely receive the support they need to reach their full potential.

Factor One: Barriers to entry remain low. Let's face it: The barriers to entry to becoming a commercial real estate agent are low. Although we like to call ourselves professionals, only a few of our fellow practitioners qualify for the formal definition (similar to a doctor, CPA, or lawyer): multiple degrees from accredited institutions, years of internship or apprentice-like training, ongoing performance certification, etc. Comparatively, a commercial real estate agent only has to be licensed by the state authority (after completion of a 60–80 hour course) and meet a few other requirements (resident of the state for a year, high school diploma, no recent arrests, etc.).

Some brokerage firms maintain minimum standards for potential agents and are quite selective in their hiring. Some offer a basic form of training. Simultaneously, though, some commercial firms have already adopted a "salon" approach: We have fifty agents associated with the firm, we have twenty desks (so get in early if you want to use one); you can use the conference room whenever it is available; you pay a monthly association fee of $450 and a per-transaction processing fee of $180 when you make a deal. After that, you get to keep whatever you earn. Good luck!

Does this sound like the barrier is getting higher? It doesn't to me.

Because of this low-barrier-to-entry approach, a wide variety of skills, attitudes, and aptitudes exists in the national pool of commercial real estate agents. The tribal folklore approach to training is essentially the only common coaching method available to most agents.

You can verify this for yourself. The National Association of Realtors recently estimated that there are approximately 120,000 commercial real estate agents in the U.S. How many agents do you know (or have even heard of) who have been professionally trained?

Here's the obvious conclusion: *If you want to consistently succeed in this industry, you have to tune out most of the noise.* You will have to ignore the behavior of most of the agents around you.

Factor Two: No sales managers = no training. In 1980, Congress passed a sweeping law that deregulated many financial institutions. The new law enabled savings and loan institutions to enter the arena of commercial real estate financing (after over 100 years of financing only residential real estate) and compete directly with the commercial banks. The result was quick disaster—by 1989, the federal government had formed the Resolution Trust Company to absorb the failed savings and loan industry, which had recklessly lent more money than the underlying real estate could withstand. The RTC's job was to sort through the failure of hundreds of lenders with loan portfolios of nearly $400 billion. Through foreclosure, the RTC became the involuntary owner of thousands of commercial real estate properties. The effect on the brokerage industry was a standstill—the agents could not earn commissions for sales (even with buyers willing to solve the issues) because the RTC could not deliver the deed. This complete standstill lasted roughly three years, until about 1992. (The RTC was overhauled in 1991.) This had a devastating effect on the brokerage houses, as they undertook draconian measures to cut expenses to survive. These cuts included either laying off all non-producing managers (the sales managers) or turning them into player-coaches who had to support themselves by making commissions in addition to running the office and coaching the agents.

Prior to the RTC crisis, most brokerages saw themselves as traditional sales organizations in which the salespeople were employed and trained as part of a corporate mission. After the crisis, the brokerage firms found themselves with low expenses (which seemed positive) but few surviving producers. So, they went after any available agents with "split": "Come to our shop and we will pay you 60%—no, wait, 70%, of the gross commissions you generate." They rationalized that these sturdy survivors didn't need a sales manager because they had endured such an arduous journey through the crisis. The brokerage firm could keep expenses low, supervise a squadron of highly incentivized salespeople with a player-coach as the "managing broker," and focus on volume now that the market was open for business again. This was the end of the sales manager era in our industry.

Looking back, we can see now that this was a short-sighted solution. It worked temporarily during the recovery period, but it has left a huge void for the generation that came after—your generation. You would be hard pressed to find a salesperson in your market today who was mentored by a trained, non-producing sales manager.

I was at CBRE for most of the 1980s, when almost every office had two non-producing managers and the split was 50–50 up to production of $1,000,000 in gross commissions. This was a common commission structure in those days. Today, a much more favorable commission split is typical: A new agent is often launched at a 60–40 split, and can move to 75–25 when the agent's gross production exceeds, say, $300,000. In other words, you have no one to help you earn these fees, but if you make them, you get to keep a much larger share than ever before.

Here's the obvious conclusion: *A higher split is not a substitute for a sales manager.* You're going to have to reckon with the question of how you are going to be coached—and pay for it yourself.

Factor Three: In the absence of training, some agents rely on relentless prospecting. As salespeople grasped the implications of a high-split, low-management approach, some of them bailed out immediately. The high split was meaningless without a plan to achieve it. However, some of the salespeople reacted as if they had struck gold. (Maybe they had; what other industry pays its salespeople so well?) They became sales addicts—they never stopped working because the commission fix was so pure and so strong. They chased every deal and relentlessly called prospects, often to the point of exhaustion (on the part of the prospect). One young agent told me that he was instructed to make 100 calls a day, and "always be sure to hang up first so that you maintain emotional control of the call. You can't let the prospects get you down."

The incomes of the goldminers soared, and the stories of their work ethic became epic tales of determination. Some agents slept in their car, or in the office, or took the train into the office with a headlamp on to read in the early morning darkness. I knew an agent who went home for dinner and baths for the kids, and then drove back to the office. These agents worked liked feverish goldminers, believing they had to extract every ounce of gold before someone else got it. It was (and still is) an impressive show of sheer force of will.

These goldminers added teammates whenever they could find any that could keep up. Their territories and their reputations reached national proportions. Today, they are held up as the heroes of the industry and are natural role models for the average agent. But—there is a problem with their example.

In my experience, even the successful goldminers will admit to giant, permanent sacrifices they've made to achieve this success. At a recent national sales conference, I heard an agent sitting in on a presentation by one of the most famous goldminers say, "I love listening to this guy talk, but I would never want his life. He makes a ton of money, but he's been divorced twice, is never home, and doesn't have any hobbies. I want more out of life than that."

Many producers claim to reject the all-or-nothing approach of a goldminer, but they have really only watered it down. They make some number of reasonable calls and chase the deals that have at least some merit. They haven't built a plan to fully penetrate a trade area and become the go-to advisor. Instead, they just suffice with being a B-player when compared to the legend.

Here's the obvious conclusion: *You could try the sheer force of will approach (because it occasionally works as long as you are willing to make the sacrifices), but there is a more sustainable path to enduring success.*

Factor Four: Independent contractor status does not favor the agent. As agent incomes began to rise in the "low expense" environment of the early 1990s, the brokerage owners balked at the amount of payroll taxes and concurrent benefit costs they had to pay for their increasingly highly paid employees. They also knew that they were managing their salespeople with a much thinner executive staff, and that ensuring agent behavior was essentially impossible. As a result, there was an industry-wide shift toward an independent contractor (IC) relationship. This wasn't a shock, really—the residential real estate industry has always operated under this structure.

This IC status implies that an agent's success is up to the agent. The employer offers a basic platform from which to operate, and the agent agrees to a certain set of conditions flowing from the platform. However, the agent cannot be told when to work, forced to come to a meeting, or even required to share information. Over time, this relationship has evolved into an indifferent partnership. As long as both sides observe the rules, they can coexist peacefully. The house covers expenses and ekes out a profit margin in the 15% range, and the agent "eats what he kills." Harmony appears to exist in most firms, but proof of the indifferent relationship is easily seen—agents change firms frequently. Top agents are often rewarded with huge bonuses to change, and sometimes change again when the bonus expires.

Ideally, the relationship would be an interdependent partnership: as the agent's income rises, the house profit rises, too. The brokerage house would logically seek to propel the agent's opportunities, skills, and technologies since it viewed the agent's revenues as return on investment. The agent would constantly seek to expand the reach of the house since the full weight of the house would be more compelling than the reputation or capabilities of just a single agent. Right?

Not really. Today, most agents simply do not measure the value of the platform that is offered. They should be wondering, *What should the house provide for its take of 40%, or at 25% when my commissions increase? How could the house help me the most? What is the value of the services that are provided?*

Here's the obvious conclusion: Although some agents are in sync with their agencies, most are not. *To maximize the value of your brokerage platform, you are going to have to reinvent your relationship with the firm, and refuse to lapse into indifference.*

YOU CAN CHOOSE TO OVERCOME THESE RESTRAINTS

The factors I've just detailed for you are still in effect. If you simply go with the flow, you will suffer the same fate that your predecessors have: no coaching, no plan, no sustainable business model. You'll simply repeat the performance of the agents before you.

In the following pages, I will teach you how to change your future by changing your perception. If you implement the prescriptions in this book, you will transform your mentality from that of a mere independent contractor associated with a brokerage firm to a focused, effective operator of a small business on a brokerage platform that propels you toward success.

You already run your own business; you just don't see it yet. By accepting a role as an independent contractor associated with a brokerage company, you've already made the choice to run a business. Your only choice now is to run it well or poorly.

Go ask the guy sitting in the manager's chair. He's running the brokerage house as a business, and he'll likely be pleased to enlighten you. He already knows that you run your own business, even if you haven't yet grasped this fundamental fact.

It is time for you to take total responsibility for all aspects of this business that you run.

To make this transformation, we'll work together from where you are to where you want to be. As you turn the pages, you'll recognize yourself in some, or maybe all, of the scenarios that I have painted. Dive in, and sift the information I present.

I've developed these prescriptions from an entire adult life spent in the commercial real estate industry. I studied the industry in school, I worked for the largest companies in the industry, I started my own firms (and learned much from both success and failure), and I've coached some of the top producers in the industry. I earned a lot of money as an agent, as a manager, and as an owner of commercial real estate. It's fair to say that my prescriptions have been hard earned.

Each chapter in the book is set up with the same formula: a pain followed by a diagnosis and a prescription. I wrote it this way so you could quickly move to the "pains" that affect you. I'll help you understand the issues, develop a new perspective, and self-medicate accordingly. If the pain fits, wear it! It's time for your perception to change, just like my perception changed that day in 1984.

Now the choice is up to you: Will you make me your "old school" sales manager, and build the career you could have? Will you let me show you how to build a sustainable business model that yields high income and the time to enjoy it?

THRIVE: PART ONE

BECOME A DOMINANT FORCE

CHAPTER 1

PROSPECTING ISN'T FUN, AND I'M ALREADY TOO BUSY

Prescription: Use a simple, top-of-mind system to maximize your prospecting

THE PAIN

As you sit in the sales meeting vaguely listening to the new guy recount the results of his prospecting over the past two weeks, you stifle a yawn.

After the meeting, the manager approaches you. "Hey, I noticed you were doodling in the meeting when Mark was giving his prospect report. Was that because you don't care about him or because prospecting, in general, is not interesting to you?"

His comments catch you off guard. After a few seconds of reflection, you reply. "Sorry, boss. I didn't mean to be disrespectful to Mark, and I do care about his success. I can't really say why I'm so indifferent to prospecting. Honestly, the fun went out of cold calling a long time ago. Most of those calls were fruitless, and I'm not motivated to pound away. Frankly, I get most of my prospects these days from leads that people feed me."

You start to add that you are really busy these days anyway, and that prospecting would only add to your workload. You stop yourself—you recognize it as an excuse before you say it out loud.

> **Deep in your heart, you know you have to prospect on a regular basis.**

Deep in your heart, you know you have to prospect on a regular basis. No one has ever shown you a simple and systematic approach that works. Every couple of years, you get slightly motivated and schedule blocks of time for prospecting. Within a few days, though, the lack of traction discourages you, and you eventually schedule over the appointments with yourself and move on.

I'm busy now. I'll probably be busy then. I'll be okay.

THE DIAGNOSIS

In the 1890s, Ivan Pavlov noticed that his dogs salivated when he came into the room. Before he could even get their food in their bowl and on the floor, the dogs were completely ready to eat. He started ringing a bell when he fed the dogs, and he could cause them to salivate just by ringing the bell. You've seen it in your own kitchen—when the can opener comes out of the drawer, the cat runs in. This immediate response to stimuli is called classical conditioning.

The sales cycle in commercial real estate is "anti-Pavlovian." It is excruciatingly long. A lot of pieces have to come together for a deal to be consummated. Agents who carefully track their deals often comment that the commission check can take more than a year to arrive after a deal is initiated. By the time the check arrives, it is completely disassociated with the prospecting effort that launched the transaction. As a result, there seems to be almost no reward to prospecting; it is the opposite of classical conditioning. Even if you have a great call, and the prospect instantly agrees to move to the next step, it is likely to be months before you get paid.

This is what has happened to you. Essentially, you've discounted the future because it seems so far away. You are in an environment that is almost completely consuming on a daily basis. The authors of *The 4 Disciplines of Execution* call this chaotic, demanding, everything-is-urgent battlefront "the whirlwind." There is so much to do right now. You've been distracted from thinking about the future. You've lapsed into a "someday, I'm going to do something about that" strategy.

Prospecting is an investment plan in which you deposit calls today for future gain. You invest time in a call today, knowing that it has a low chance of immediate gain. Depositing prospect calls in a systematic fashion grows into new deals somewhere down the road. It pays off in the future. Your father faithfully contributed to his investment plan, and that plan paid off when he was able to pay for a big share of your college costs. You are a direct beneficiary of a "regular deposit investment" plan; you deeply appreciate the outcome.

The chances of calling on a prospect at the exact moment he needs you are extremely low.

But these are the days of instant gratification and, darn it, the adrenaline rush of being in battle is addictive. The whirlwind is just too gratifying right now!

THE PRESCRIPTION

Let's get you back in the savings business. The solution is a simple-to-use, highly logical prospecting system. I call it the top-of-mind system. I didn't invent it, but I have spent a lot of years adapting it to our industry.

Here is the basic premise: The chances of calling on a prospect at the exact moment he needs you are extremely low. However, if you occupy the top-of-mind slot in his brain associated with "trusted commercial real estate advisor," he will call you when he is ready.

What does *top of mind* mean? Try this experiment: when I say the product, you say the first brand that comes into your mind. Ready?

Pickup truck: _____
Blue jeans: _____
Toothpaste: _____
Beer: _____
Cigarette: _____

You said Marlboro, didn't you? How do you explain that? You don't even smoke, and you named that brand without hesitation. That's the meaning of *top of mind*.

Think about the beer you named for a moment. Why does the manufacturer continue to advertise so heavily when they already occupy a top-of-mind slot in the minds of so many people? That slot must be valuable!

Now imagine that you assemble 125 people in an auditorium. Each of them is a player in your trade area. I take the stage and explain the top-of-mind exercise. I announce a product, and they shout back the brand that comes to mind first. It goes quickly. This time, though, after cigarette, I say "trusted commercial real estate advisor." How many of the 125 would shout your name?

I've asked more than 100 successful agents that question. The agents usually guess that somewhere between 10 and 40 people would name them first. What is your number, right now?

How much money do you think you would you make if all 125 people named you first? Seriously. Let's do the math. If you made

$250,000 last year having only 10 people who would name you first, that equates to $25,000 per person. Hmmm. 125 people would equate to . . . a very large number!

There's your entire prospecting system. It is simple, and it works. Your job is to choose 125 people and make enough top-of-mind deposits that they eventually call you. Who should you choose? There are only two criteria:

1. They must be willing to eventually interact with you. If they will not take your call, or are already committed to someone else, or hate salespeople, they don't qualify. Sometimes it takes a year to figure this out. Replace them with someone else.

2. They will get pregnant at least once every five years. By "pregnant," I mean they will give birth to a deal that you want to control at least once over the next five years. They may control the deal or they may be an influencer, but either way, they would be in a position to potentially award the deal to you.

If you spread these 125 deals out evenly over the next five years, 25 deals controlled by your target audience would be awarded every year. If you occupied the top-of-mind slot in the brain of the person awarding those deals, how many of the annual deals do you think you could capture? Twenty percent (five deals)? Forty percent (10 deals)? Sixty percent (15 deals)? All of them?

If you captured, say, 10 deals per year every year, this would essentially equate to a salary. If the average deal was worth, say, $25,000, you would have an annual salary of $250,000. Any money you earned from unplanned events would just be unlimited bonuses on top of your salary.

You can calculate your own math, but my experience is that the math works pretty well with 125 targets. But what really attracts me is the simplicity of the prospecting effort. The magic number of 125 works on that front, too. Here's how:

> *There are 13 weeks in a quarter; suppose you work 12 weeks per quarter. (The other week is allocated to holidays and time off.) That means you have 60 work days each quarter. If you make a high-quality connection with 2 of your 125 targets every day, you'll work through your entire roster of 125 targets in a quarter. If you repeat this every quarter, you'll make 4 significant connections in a year with each of your targeted prospects.*

Think of these connecting "touches" as quarterly deposits in their top-of-mind bank. Do you believe that four meaningful communications per year for five years would earn the top-of-mind slot?

How many hours per day would it take to make two significant touches? (A "significant touch" means a conversation, not an email blast or a voicemail message. The fingerprint evidence of a significant touch is that you learned something during the conversation. You might have learned that he's more interested in leasing than buying, that his daughter goes to Notre Dame, or that the CFO, Susan Travers, has an important role in real estate decisions.) Would it take 20 minutes? An hour?

Once you've made your two touches for the day, take the rest of the day off. What the heck—you've earned your salary, haven't you? Or you can re-enter the whirlwind or chase the lead you were given or call on the guy in the building next to your listing. Remember, you are free to earn those unlimited bonuses, too.

By the way, the tone of your touches will not sound like a prospecting call. Remember—you are not attempting to call him on exactly the right day. Because you are only making deposits so he will call you, your tone is relaxed and consultative. This is the opposite of churning. ("Hi. Do you want to sell? No? Thanks. Bye.") You should be alert to his needs and inquire about opportunities to work together, but you don't have to push. Pushing wears out both of you, and does not make the "trusted commercial real estate advisor" label appear in his brain.

The system is simple to operate. It does not require a massive database or a multifaceted CRM. You can operate this system on one spreadsheet. Many of my clients simply use columns for the quarterly contact next to each name on the list. Sometimes, we turn it into a game: 0 points for no contact, 1 point for a voicemail exchange (the prospect has to call you back), 3 points for a phone conversation, and 5 points for a face-to-face meeting. We track a very simple goal—earn 250 points per quarter.

The authors of *The 4 Disciplines of Execution* suggest that a game can be extremely motivating, especially when you add a scoreboard that all team members view on a regular basis. No one wants to come to a meeting and see that they are lagging behind; they want to march up to the scoreboard and slap their number on the board for everyone to see. This is essentially what happens to me when I open a coaching call with a client, and he immediately says, "Let's start today by looking at the scoreboard."

Here's your first prescription: a simple-to-use, easy-to-operate, minimal-time-requirement prospecting system that pays a salary. Pretty sweet, eh?

ONE MORE THING

It's okay. You can tell people that you don't cold call. I don't think a senior producer in your position should be cold calling. At this point, all of your calls should be warm calls.

If you were just starting in the business, cold calling would be the only strategy available. Why should you reduce yourself to the same system a rookie uses? How does cold calling distinguish you from a much lesser competitor?

You already know that if the rookie survives, he will get busy and stop prospecting, anyway. There's no need for you to battle with him; he will eventually take himself out of the game, as almost every salesperson does.

It is not okay to have no savings plan. Choose 125 VIPs and commit yourself to a systematic calling plan. Dominance lies in your future!

CHAPTER 2

I HAVE MORE PROJECTS THAN I CAN MANAGE

Prescription: Use the tool that professional project managers use—a Gantt chart

THE PAIN

The good news is that you have a lot of projects underway. The bad news is that you have a lot of projects underway. Your team has never been so successful. Your reputation and results have earned you the opportunity to perform on more assignments than you have ever attempted before. However, since you've never managed so many projects simultaneously, you are in serious danger of dropping the ball on one or all of them.

This is not child's play. You have committed to a rigorous schedule on each project. You believe your team can handle each project because you've handled similar projects before. You are counting on your teammates to perform as they have in the past—and as you have promised the client. It occurs to you, though, that making a mistake or breaking a promise on one or more of these projects could be both embarrassing and costly.

Last night, you lay awake wondering about the progress on each project. You realized that you have to manage all of the details more effectively. Although you trust your team, you need some serious accountability. The only thing you can think to do is send out multiple emails asking for an update. You felt a little bit better this morning but came into the office to find nervous and edgy teammates.

Nobody likes getting midnight emails, Bud. Would you like to sit down and talk about the projects I am running, or force me into a long reply to your email?

THE DIAGNOSIS

It is true that these are large and important projects—especially to your clients. They interviewed several agents and chose you because they believe you can perform. They are really counting on you. The memory of the client's comment as he awarded the project to you still rings in your ears: "Hey, do a good job for us. But remember, this is not a matter of life and death—it's much more important than that." He was smiling, but he wasn't laughing.

> **It is time to acknowledge that you are now a professional project manager.**

It is time to acknowledge that you are now a professional project manager. When lots of money, people, and responsibilities are involved, professionals take over. These projects meet these criteria: Millions of dollars will be invested, many people will be stakeholders in the decisions, and your team has the responsibility of guiding all of the interests to a successful conclusion.

Professional project managers use powerful tools. A professional pilot or ship's captain would never leave port without filing a detailed plan for the voyage. What plan have you implemented for your projects? How are all of the team members, including the client, able to understand the plan you have created and the progress made to date? Is your plan still on track?

THE PRESCRIPTION

Take heart—this is not a new problem, and powerful solutions exist. Henry Gantt resolved this issue more than 100 years ago. He created the Gantt chart to organize any project with multiple components. Perhaps without realizing it, you have seen a Gantt chart before. If you have ever been in a construction trailer, you were within inches of a Gantt chart.

Every commercial building you have ever leased or sold was constructed using a Gantt chart. Every contractor uses a Gantt chart to control the project's cost and delivery. There is simply no other way to ensure that the pipes are laid after the foundation is set but before the slab is poured. A Gantt chart was used even if the project consisted only of installing tenant improvements in an existing building. Think about it—if it takes a Gantt chart to construct or renovate a building, doesn't it make sense that a Gantt chart would be valuable in marketing it?

> **Henry Gantt resolved this issue more than 100 years ago.**

If you are unfamiliar with the Gantt chart, simply research it online. There are thousands of sample Gantt charts for you to view, and you can easily sample the software used to create a Gantt chart. Try this simple exercise: take a blank sheet of paper and a marker, and draw your own Gantt chart for hard-boiling an egg. You'll quickly see how the chart helps you manage the interrelationship of all of the necessary steps.

The basics of a Gantt chart can be learned at www.gantt.com. Any university that teaches construction courses will have a basic scheduling class that may work for you. The most popular Gantt chart creator is Microsoft Project. Like Microsoft Excel, it is massively powerful and has features beyond what you will ever use. The basics of Project are manageable, though, and can be learned from Microsoft, Lynda.com, and other online tutorials at low cost. Many other software programs are available. Ask professional contractors what Gantt chart software they use and why. You'll find the one that works best for you.

Once you become familiar with a Gantt chart, you will quickly begin to understand these benefits of using a Gantt chart for your projects:

1. **A Gantt chart demonstrates that you understand the total scope of the project, the sequence of the tasks, the duration of each task, the precursors for each task, and the time required to complete the entire project.** The precursors are the prior elements that must be in place before the next task can commence. Think in terms of filing the plans in order to get the building permit in order to break ground.

2. **There is no more effective demonstration of your experience than a Gantt chart. As you walk the client through the project schedule, he quickly grasps that you have done this many times before.** You'll find that using a Gantt chart in your listing presentation is distinctive and compelling. I've challenged agents to see if they could get a listing with only a one page presentation—a Gantt chart. Try it.

3. **A Gantt chart creates a set of common expectations for the project. The client can see the entire story in one glance.** He doesn't have to wonder what you are doing. The chart shows him what to expect on any given day. I like to install a task for every time I will

report to the client. Instead of agreeing to report every two weeks, I report at designated plateaus in the project schedule.

4. **One of the most useful elements of a Gantt chart is to show the prospect where his involvement is needed.** As an example, if the marketing materials require his approval prior to printing, he can anticipate receiving the materials and knows how long he has to make decisions. One of my favorite moments in a Gantt chart presentation is when I say, "Now Mr. Jones, as you can see, we've allotted four days in Task #16 for you to approve the marketing materials. Will this work for you? If not, it is okay—I will adjust the final completion date to give you the time you need." When he sees that his task is part of the critical path, he will be eager to comply with the schedule.

5. **Another customer-centric benefit of using a Gantt chart is displaying the responsibilities of each team member.** Each task line can be assigned to a team member, and even color-coded for clarity. Imagine yourself saying to Mr. Jones, "We take a very specific team approach to this project. I am responsible for lines 1–4, 12, 15, and 22–26. Jessica is responsible for lines 5–8, 11, 13, and 16–21. Bill is responsible for all of the other lines, except the three that are assigned to you."

   Incidentally, this parsing of the project into individual lines of responsibility enables you to build tremendous competence among your team members. As your teammates repeatedly work on the same task groups, they become experts. This further differentiates you from your competition and enhances your service to the client.

6. **Gantt charts enable you to manage your projects with greater continuity. Over time, you will learn to install expansion joints**

into the schedule. This enables you to deliver on the promised date, even as tasks inevitably swell and shrink. Imagine a contractor with a hard delivery date—wouldn't he have learned to install nuggets of extra time to account for almost certain rain delays and material shortages?

7. **A Gantt chart helps you support your commission stance. When you craft a Gantt chart, you'll realize how much work your team really performs** ("Wow! We do a lot more than I thought. Given that we only get paid at the end if everything goes right, we're worth every penny we're charging.") If the client asks for a lower fee, point to the Gantt chart. "Hmm. I wonder what steps we could eliminate to achieve the lower fee and yet still get the job done." A surgeon once told me that when he is asked to lower his fee, he usually responds with, "Well, I guess we could eliminate the anesthesia."

8. **The greatest single benefit of using a Gantt chart for each project is being able to mastermind all of the simultaneous projects.** Imagine yourself entering a team meeting in which each project is displayed on a Gantt chart. You would be able to zoom in on each project's progress very quickly as you view its Gantt chart. ("This is where we are supposed to be today. Are we there? Will we be ready for the next step in three more days? What help do you need from me at this point?") Within a very short time, you would be able to make crucial decisions and focus on the most significant challenges. By the time the meeting was over, you would be up to speed on all projects. You'll enjoy peace of mind, knowing the status of hundreds of details. No need for the midnight email tonight.

Remember the whirlwind—the chaos that awaits you after you finish crafting your Gantt chart? When you take the time to manufacture a

Gantt chart, the project is essentially under control. You just have to execute the details you've planned. That means you can go back into the whirlwind and be present—because your head is clear, and your plans are already underway.

The next time you drive by a property under construction in your trade area, take a moment to reflect. Somewhere, a young project manager is bent over his Gantt chart, carefully plotting his priorities. Somewhere else, an architect and an engineer are in their offices at the same moment, scrutinizing a Gantt chart for their roles in the same project.

Someday you'll sell that property. Go ahead and say it: "Thank you, Mr. Gantt, for enabling these professionals to create this future inventory for me and my team. I've decided to honor you by using your chart to convey the property from their client to mine."

ONE MORE THING

One of the first decisions you'll have to make when you start a new Gantt chart is what unit of time to employ. You can select hours, week days, calendar days, weeks, months, quarters—or even years.

The largest Gantt chart I've ever seen filled the entire wall in a large hallway. The unit of time that had been selected was seconds. There were more than 200 task lines. The chart's legend showed that 15 people were responsible for one or more of the tasks.

What was the subject of this Gantt chart? Childbirth.

In other words, if you were born in the last 40 years, you were born under the sign of Gantt. If you were born more than 40 years ago, the Gantt chart was probably only in the mind of the attending physician.

Either way, you might as well acknowledge your heritage—a Gantt chart is in your DNA. You owe your very existence to a Gantt chart. It seems like the least you could do to honor your forefather is to create a Gantt chart occasionally.

CHAPTER 3

TOO MUCH TIME GETS WASTED ON DEALS THAT FALL APART IN THE END

Prescription: Employ a masterful due-diligence process as if you were a principal

THE PAIN

You remember the last time you realized you had wasted time on a deal that didn't materialize. You were almost nauseated. You promised yourself you would avoid this situation in the future. Never again. But—it's happening again. What went wrong?

It's been more than nine months since you made your listing presentation. It took five months to get the property under contract. By contract specifications, the deal is supposed to close in the next 30 days. Instead, the buyer's due-diligence effort uncovered a problem that hasn't gone away. The parties are starting to bark threats at each other. The next email will probably convey the ultimatum from the seller, which the buyer has already promised to refuse.

As you ponder the chronology of the deal, trying to figure out what has gone wrong and how the problem could have been avoided, you recall the seller telling you that he didn't think there were any problems with the property. "At least, not major ones," he said.

You remember riffling through the bundle of documents the seller gave you, most of which were created at the time of his purchase ten years ago. The seller resisted when you suggested updating the survey prior to taking the property to market. He took the position that the buyer will determine what he needs in order to close during the due-diligence period. "I'll give the buyer 45 days of free look to study anything he wants. Hey, man, it's a *caveat emptor* world out there. Buyer beware, baby. I had to do the same thing when I bought the property." You shrugged it off and moved ahead with the marketing, assuming he was probably right.

That strategy has backfired. The buyer is a veteran and showed you the 6-page due-diligence checklist he uses. Not surprisingly, he found three major issues. Two of them have been resolved, but the third issue is more complicated; it will take significant time and money to implement the fix. Unfortunately, the parties have hardened in their positions, now that money is at risk. It is not looking good.

We're going to lose this deal. I can feel it coming.

THE DIAGNOSIS

You have accurately assessed the situation. Despite having two "ready, willing and able" parties at the table, the deal is about to collapse. The buyer wants more time and a reduction in price. The seller is resisting, although he has floated the idea of reducing the commission to pay for some of these newfound expenses.

Despite your years of experience, you feel foolishly caught (again!) in an argument that probably could have been avoided. Bad luck? A wrinkle in the karma? Full moon?

You are a professional project manager now. Did you use all of your experience to anticipate potential problems? Did you proactively manage expectations? Does it make sense to you now that you relied on the opposing party to identify problems with your property? Could the problems that were uncovered have been identified and resolved in advance?

Think back to that time when you sold your first car. You washed it, vacuumed it, put the shiny stuff on the tires and changed the oil to get the new sticker on the windshield. You assembled all of the records and put them in a brand new manila envelope. Why?

You wanted the buyer to see that the car was in good shape, had been properly maintained, and was ready for its new owner. You wanted to achieve the price you set. You wanted to sell the car quickly. And you did—for $4,500 to the second guy who looked at it. You got it done in one Saturday morning. You handled that project like a pro!

If it works for a used car, should this same strategy be used for a multi-million dollar property?

THE PRESCRIPTION

If you are going to take listings, represent the seller, and get paid on a commission basis, you must make every effort to drive the due-diligence process in advance. Since you are using a Gantt chart now, install the due-diligence tasks as line items in the listing presentation. Force the discussion with the seller. Emphasize that controlling the due-diligence process greatly increases the chances that you can deliver

> **Since you are using a Gantt chart now, install the due-diligence tasks as line items in the listing presentation.**

the project as shown in the Gantt chart. The buyer will still have a due-diligence period, but it can be shorter and less uncertain if you know what to expect. The alternative is to stop the chart at the point at which the buyer's due-diligence study period begins and say, "We'll just have to see how it goes."

There are several compelling reasons to take control of the due-diligence process at the outset of the listing.

1. The doctrine of *caveat emptor* is weakening in the courts. The "buyer beware" pendulum is swinging toward the buyer in the commercial arena, just as it has in the residential arena. Sellers of commercial real estate have increasing responsibility to disclose issues (even suspected issues) to the buyer. The doctrine doesn't work to the seller's benefit anyway—when a buyer uncovers an issue, he prices the solution at a premium price because he assumes that the problem is even bigger than it is. He may adopt a pessimistic attitude about the property in general ("I wonder what else is wrong that I don't know about?") that will only work against the seller as the deal progresses.

    If a seller has the property inspected and receives a report, he will have to give the report to the buyer. You could view this as potentially revealing flaws that might not have been found or might not matter to the buyer. Or, you could use the report to say, "Here is our inspection report. The major issues have already been addressed, and the remainder has been accounted for in the price. We expect this report to shorten your own review."

    Appropriate, expedient pricing considerations can be made by the seller in advance. The seller may choose to address a flaw by a change in pricing. As an example, the seller may state up front that he is offering a $50,000 credit at closing for a leaky roof, instead of replacing it. Most buyers prefer this so that they can control the selection, quality, and price of the new roof. The alternative would be for the seller to fix the problem—which will extend the contract while the seller finds a roofer, installs the roof, and waits through the inspection by the buyer's roofer.

2. A serious seller will have evaluated the market carefully. The seller believes that this is the right time in the cycle to sell the property. Accordingly, once the decision is made to sell, he wants to execute quickly. *The single greatest influence the seller can have on the closing schedule is to manage the due-diligence process.* Even a low price doesn't cause a quicker close—very few buyers will put their name in the chain of title on a mystery package just because the price was so attractive.

    If the seller is selling due to hardship or divorce instead of cyclical reasons, the timing is even more acute. The need for advance due diligence is even greater in these cases. The only sellers who are indifferent to timing are the ones looking for a free appraisal.

3. Professional buyers want to close quickly, too. They've made the decision that the property fulfills a goal for them, and now they want to execute as soon as possible. Professional buyers appreciate receiving a seller's inspection report and respect the effort of the seller to transfer the property quickly and professionally.

    If the buyer wants to argue over an issue that was disclosed up front, perhaps the buyer is not serious or hasn't fully assembled the funds to close. You may find that you can take a harder line with this buyer in the negotiations, since he may not be real.

4. When the inevitable issues arise during the contract negotiations, a seller who has performed the due diligence in advance has a team of consultants already assembled. If the buyer were to raise the issue of title or survey or leaky roof or groundwater contamination, the consultant who studied the effort for the seller is immediately available

to respond. This means that the seller brings his own expert to the table and enhances the probability that the issues will be dealt with inside the contract timing.

Aren't these just more sophisticated versions of the same steps you took when you sold your car?

ONE MORE THING

You are a stakeholder in this transaction as well as the buyer and seller. If the deal does not close, the seller still has the property and the buyer still has his cash. You, however, cannot recover all of the effort that you invested. Your assets are time and expertise, and you just invested them for free.

Putting it bluntly: Ensuring that the seller undertakes an appropriate due-diligence process prior to offering the property for sale increases the probability that the deal will close and you will get paid.

Why not get in front of this issue? When I show the due-diligence line items on my Gantt chart (see Chapter 2), I explain that I will manage them for a moderate fee, paid in advance. I then deduct the fee from the commission at closing. I explain that I traffic in the due-diligence arena every day. I have developed relationships with consultants who are fast, thorough, and focused on solutions. I insist that the vendors take a proprietary approach ("What would you do if this were your property?"). Because I represent repeat business to them, the price they charge me is less than what they would charge the seller.

> **You are a stakeholder in this transaction as well as the buyer and seller.**

The seller recovers more than the fee I charge for due diligence due to the vendor cost savings I deliver.

This approach forces the discussion with the seller. If he doesn't want high-quality/low-cost scrutiny of his property that takes very little of his time before we put it on the market, what message is he sending? If you are really determined not to waste your time, isn't this the necessary discussion you must have up front? Even if you compromise in this discussion with the seller and decide to go ahead anyway, aren't you taking a more calculated risk?

If you want to be a dominant agent, you have to work on deals that close. There is no trophy for a really great effort that didn't quite pan out.

CHAPTER 4

I SHOULD BE MUCH MORE DOMINANT IN MY NICHE

*Prescription: Invoke your "power to convene"
to become the undisputed leader*

THE PAIN

The industrial agent who sits in the adjacent cubicle waves you over. "Hey! Did you hear about the big law firm that's relocating downtown? They decided to hold a beauty pageant and interview four agents for the tenant representation assignment."

Your heart sinks. You didn't get invited. Three months ago, the same thing happened when a local family decided to sell their three office buildings. Despite your successes, you somehow didn't qualify to even propose your services. You can't get a hit if you can't get to the plate!

Something's wrong. You've put a lot of effort into building your presence in the marketplace. You've got a dozen signs in place that prominently display your name. You send more than 2,500 emails each month. You consistently post an article on the company's website. You retweet at least two articles a week. Every deal you close generates a press release that you personally send to the editor of the business journal. You are active in two trade associations, and you are a deacon at your church.

Everybody knows me, right? How come I didn't get invited to the dance?

THE DIAGNOSIS

Yep, you are well known. You've built your presence in a variety of ways, and that has earned you very high name recognition. If someone conducted the top-of-mind exercise (see Chapter 1), you might not come out on top every time, but you'd probably be named in the first five agents more than half the time.

Take a moment to think about the "power" in your presence. A lot of people know of you, but somehow it does not convert to power—the kind of power that gets you invited to beauty pageants.

The marketers might call this powerful presence by another name: *brand equity*. The ultimate brand equity is revealed when people pay more for your service or product than a competitive one. You can hear brand equity in the revered way people talk about the product. I think Big Green Egg when I think about brand equity. Customers pay about twice as much for this barbecue grill than similar ones.

In your case, brand equity might translate to status—the status that gets you mentioned in every article or merits an invitation to almost every beauty pageant.

How can you build a powerful presence that distinguishes you from the crowd?

THE PRESCRIPTION

To stand above the crowd, you have to think differently. The presence-building tactics that you've used to date have been valuable. They've generated measurable name recognition, so you haven't wasted your time and effort. But they are common tactics, and they have made you merely a recognizable name in the crowd. You're significant but not dominant.

Let's change your perspective.

- The governor calls you. He asks you to come to the state capital tomorrow to lead a committee related to commercial real estate. You'd probably go.

- Bill Gates asks you to make a presentation at his upcoming summit meeting for the billionaires club he runs. You'll be there.

- When Garth Brooks played a concert in your town and invited you to come for $65, you went—along with 75,000 of his closest friends.

These are all examples of using the "power to convene." Under Article II, Section 3, of the U.S. Constitution, The President of the United States has the power to convene Congress—he can compel them to assemble. In a less formal scenario, the power to convene flows from status (Governor) or influence (Bill Gates) or rarity (Garth Brooks). In all of these cases, you (as part of their audience) came to them. You convened when they called.

Exercising this power to convene causes a subtle power shift. When you are prospecting, you go to the prospect. You try to create a scenario in which they agree to spend time with you. When you use the power to convene, they come to you. You alter the value proposition from "If you will spend time with me, I'll work hard to make it valuable to you" to "I'm willing to share my valuable knowledge with you if you will invest effort to participate."

This shift not only affects where and when the interaction takes place, but it also changes the emotional dynamic. The prospect has now assigned tremendous value to your expertise and insight. He has physically altered his schedule to be part of your show. He wants to be influenced by you.

There are several ways that dominant agents that I know have used the power to convene. Here are some of the best:

- Host a webinar in which you explain the market condition or a new trend. Instead of sending a bland report via email, invite prospects to a vibrant 15-minute presentation. Say something interesting, and customize your remarks. The agent who uses this technique tells me that he routinely fields calls after the webinar from his prospects who have opportunities they want to discuss.

- Host the annual market forum in your market. This is old school—a lot of brokerage firms used to do this, but they now seem to have abandoned it in favor of the email blast. Yet it still works. My client assembles more than 300 people each year at his forum, and sponsors clamor to be involved. It's become the power networking function of the year in that market, and it sells out two weeks before the event.

- Take advantage of an assembled audience by making a customized presentation. I have a client who focuses on the real estate of dentists. He often makes a presentation at the semi-annual gathering of all of the CPAs in the state. (Apparently, dentists are heavily swayed by their CPAs.) The CPAs are eager to bridge the gap between the real estate market and the dentists. He is routinely invited to return, and he harvests several prospects with each appearance.

- Another client has used another old-school tactic, the lunch-n-learn, very effectively. He calls a lender and offers to update the lender's entire staff on the market. Sometimes he brings lunch; sometimes they supply it. In 45 minutes of presentation and Q&A, the client establishes his credibility. Inevitably, one of the lenders asks if he would be interested in evaluating a property that they want to "resolve."

- I'm aware of an agent who makes presentations at the team meetings of his large clients. He does work for a handful of REITs. When the REIT leadership assembles their internal team for regional staff meetings and team retreats, he pays his own way to make a presentation at their meeting. "I don't charge a fee, and I have to buy my own airline ticket, but they usually put me up at their luxury hotel and include me in their meals. It's almost like a mini-vacation for me. They're extremely interested in market trends, so I try to focus on 3–4 issues where the needle has moved since the last time they assembled. So far, I have been called in every time they consider moving a property."

How could you accelerate your presence campaign by invoking your power to convene?

ONE MORE THING

If you want to be the dominant agent in your trade area, you have to claim that spot. You could literally claim it—I am the dominant agent in the area—and use it as your tag line and in your email signature. You could paint the words on your signs and install them on your business card. That might do the trick.

It would be more effective, though, if the market voted you into that position. People vote with their feet—it's not what you say, it's what they do. Garth might call himself the most popular recording artist of all times, but the proof is in the sold-out arena.

I'm aware of an agent who created an annual tennis tournament that benefits a local charity. He puts a lot of effort into it, and the participants have a lot of fun with it. He gets a lot of love from both the participants and the charity recipients. Through the years, he has worked hard to build his audience. Because the number of players that can be on the courts at one time is small, and because he has wanted every participant to have a top-notch experience, he's kept the event limited in size. Now, the participants call him, making sure they know the date well in advance so they don't risk losing their spot.

Another agent held a real estate roundtable for many years at a private beach lodge on the Atlantic coast. There were only 16 beds, so the guest list had to be managed very carefully. He created an agenda that included relaxation in a beautiful corner of the world, great food and wine, and stimulating conversation. The attendees treasured the event each year (even though it was not easy to get there), and it wasn't long until he was turning people away.

These agents are on a higher plane when it comes to their presence campaign. They're not pushers (emails, press releases, tweets), they're conveners. Their audience votes with their feet—they come when called.

Could you be this dominant?

THRIVE: PART TWO

BUILD A TEAM

CHAPTER 5

WHY AM I WORKING ON THESE ADMINISTRATIVE TASKS? I NEED HELP!

Prescription: Use this proven process to find and employ an effective assistant

THE PAIN

It is 12:30 on Monday afternoon. You are standing at the copy machine, hand-collating copies of the proposal that you will deliver in 90 minutes. It needs one more round of editing. The proposal is only good—not great. You wish you had more time to review it and practice its delivery.

You might have had time to enhance the proposal and practice your presentation, but you promised yourself that you would log 20 new prospects into your CRM by Monday morning, which required three hours of research on the state's corporate register website. You didn't end up getting that done until Sunday afternoon. This morning, the weekly sales meeting cost you another 90 minutes.

After the sales meeting, you punched your weekend research into the CRM. There's no time to make those calls now. Over the next four hours, you will be completely consumed by getting the proposal assembled and delivered. You find yourself hoping that the prospect will ask for a week to make his decision after you present your proposal. Hopefully, you can get to the new prospect calls tomorrow.

> **How do you expect to make big money when you are working on stuff an assistant should be doing?**

You already feel stress. There is too much to do, and not enough time to do it. It's only Monday afternoon, and that familiar tension overwhelms your stomach. You try to close down that little voice in your head telling you that these are all $15-per-hour tasks. It says, "How do you expect to make big money when you're working on stuff an assistant should be doing? You don't see top producers standing at the copy machine, do you? Why aren't you practicing the proposal?"

Man, I'm not going to have time to eat again today.

THE DIAGNOSIS

You're right—you cannot average, say, $200 per hour when you are working on $15-per-hour tasks several times per day. You obviously need assistance.

The first option, of course, is to use the support staff supplied by the firm. Many times, these assistants are shared between agents and ping-pong between the highest priorities and the most demanding agents. You may even have an assistant whom you share with only one other agent. However, you often find you could do the work yourself in the amount of time it would take to explain it to a part-time assistant and then review it. As a result, even though assistance might be available, it seems more expedient to plow through the task yourself.

Often, no support is available from the firm. You have to arrange for your own support through some combination of part-time and remote assistance. This seems just as troubling as doing the work yourself—finding and managing the support requires much more effort than you wanted to invest.

It seems like an insurmountable task—finding someone to supply you with readily available, high-quality, customized support. You feel like you're stuck in a no-win situation—burdened with administrative tasks but not knowing how to find the support that you need.

Ultimately, you already understand that you cannot make any more progress without addressing this issue. The time has come to draw a line in the sand. *You must find a way to add to your team, or you will be doomed to the physical limits of your own efforts.*

Stephen Covey introduced us to his four quadrants of time management in his perennial bestseller, *The Seven Habits of Highly Effective People.* The four quadrants are part of his 3rd Habit: Put First Things First. To paraphrase Covey, if you will not venture into Quadrant II (not urgent, but important) to scrutinize and enhance your workflow processes, you will be endlessly stuck in Quadrant I (urgent and important), where the stress of continual deadlines will eventually exhaust you. Defining the role for an assistant and working through the process to find and employ the right assistant is a Quadrant II activity. When complete, it enables you to more effectively re-enter Quadrant I and focus your efforts on those $200/hour tasks.

	Urgent	Not Urgent
Important	**Quadrant I:** Urgent & Important	**Quadrant II:** Not Urgent & Important
Not Important	**Quadrant III:** Urgent & Not Important	**Quadrant IV:** Not Urgent & Not Important

THE PRESCRIPTION

Take a moment to regain some perspective. You've entered into a performance driven, commission-compensation arena. You have to focus on production. You must find a way to leverage your efforts to succeed in an environment in which you only "eat what you kill."

So how do we find the perfect assistant for you?

Here are the steps I have used with many agents to climb this mountain.

1. **Start with an organizational chart.**

    Create an org chart for your team that shows how all of the pieces fit together. Be sure to include corporate resources, part-time and remote resources, key vendors, and fellow agents in the firm, as well as your own inner circle. Now, draw in a new box that shows where your to-be-hired assistant would fit. Make sure that you could narrate to anyone who looked at the chart how the assistant would contribute to the success of the organization.

2. **List the things the assistant should do every day.**

    Think through the tasks that would be done on a daily, weekly, monthly, and quarterly basis. List each task on a separate line. Be sure all of the tasks you detest are on the list. Show the list to a teammate to ensure that the list is as complete as possible.

3. **In light of the tasks listed, what skills and attributes are imperative for this role?**

    Be as specific as possible in listing the attributes. As an example, if the tasks reveal that there are many lists to be updated on a regular basis, the attribute might be "strong attention to detail," and the skill might be "demonstrable ability to prioritize." If the role requires expertise in Microsoft Excel, what specific functions must be accomplished by the assistant (e.g., basic math operations, presentation-level formatting, graphing, pivot tables, calculation of internal rate of return, etc.)? If the role requires interaction with the public, does the assistant have to be willing and able to talk comfortably with people he or she does not know?

4. **Develop an interview scorecard.**

    Now that you understand where the job fits in your organization, the role the assistant will play, and the attributes that must be present, you are almost ready to start interviewing candidates. The key to effective interviewing, though, is to have an interview scorecard. This document enables you to focus your interview time on the most important factors. A weak interview question would be, "Are you good at Excel?" or "How would you rate your Excel skills?" A much stronger question would be, "If I asked you to convert a spreadsheet showing vacancy in several submarkets into a graph that would be inserted into PowerPoint, what would be your first step?"

    Alternatively, if you were seeking to understand the ability to prioritize, you could ask, "Are you an organized person?" Or you could ask, "How do you keep track of your daily task list? What happens if there are more tasks than there are hours to complete them?"

    As you work through the interview with a candidate, you can grade the candidate according to the strength of their answers to very specific questions. If you ask all of the candidates approximately the same questions, you can choose the best candidates from the pool.

5. **Find candidates from a variety of sources, and interview at least three candidates.**

    You can look for candidates in a variety of ways. The most common is to use the online resources (LinkedIn, Indeed, ZipRecruiter, etc.). This is simply a matter of paying the fee and posting the job description. These tools will enable you to assemble a pool fairly quickly.

In addition, I recommend that you also send the job description to a handful of friends and close associates, asking them to review the job description and recommend anyone who comes to mind. You can also post the job description in trade association newsletters, university career centers, and other membership organizations.

Close the sourcing period when you have a reasonable pool of candidates. Sift through the applications you have received, and pick out at least three attractive candidates. Use your interview scorecard to zero in on the most qualified candidate.

6. **Use additional resources to complement the interviews.**

    You may choose to have other people interview the candidates, and use third-party natural behavior assessments as part of your evaluation. Do not hesitate to use specific tests to add to your understanding of the candidate's skills. As an example, offer the candidate a laptop with a spreadsheet on the screen, and ask them to undertake specific tasks. I know one interviewer who asks the candidate to scrutinize a spreadsheet and find the errors. I've asked many candidates to come to an interview after carefully reviewing the company's website. I tell them to come to the interview with three suggestions on how we could make the website more effective.

    When you feel that you are getting close, ask the candidate for a list of references. Sometimes, the names on the list will surprise you. Ask why the candidate chose the people on the list, and if the most recent employers are included. Be sure that the list you are given includes name, role, contact information, and the relationship of the parties. Call the references. It's easy to "fall in love" with a candidate.

Reference checks can keep you from making a bad hiring decision. I like to ask a reference this question: "If I were to call you five years from now and thank you for recommending this candidate because they have done a great job for us, why would you not be surprised?"

The best candidate will emerge as you consider their background, past experiences, interview responses, third-party assessments, skills tests, and reference testimonials.

7. **Develop the template for the 90-day review.**

There is one more tool I like to use in the interview process. Assuming you're willing to give your new assistant feedback on his or her performance, go ahead and craft the form you will use for the 90-day review. Working through this process will help you connect the dots from the interview scorecard to the actual performance you expect. I like to show the 90-day review form to the top candidates in the interview process and ask them if they feel they could earn a high rating. Sometimes, their answer can be the final, compelling stroke in my decision-making process.

ONE MORE THING

When I describe this process to my clients, I hear an occasional sigh. "This just seems like a lot of work," they exclaim. I agree—it is a lot of work. Once complete, though, this assistant can lead you to a level of productivity you have never experienced before. If you are already at full capacity, this is your only option.

You can work through this process yourself or outsource it. At worst, you might interview just one candidate and go with your gut. In any case, when you get to the moment of decision, ask yourself this question: What specific skills does this person have that will accelerate my personal production?

Please don't hire an assistant to merely absorb the items that you want to delegate. Instead, think offensively—how can this person cause me to be more productive? What would you want to be able to say if, one year from now, you were asked, "How has your assistant enabled you to achieve your goals?"

CHAPTER 6

I HAVE AN ASSISTANT, BUT IT IS NOT WORKING (AGAIN)

Prescription: Turn your assistant into an accelerator for your business

THE PAIN

Okay, Blaine. I followed your advice; no more $15-per-hour tasks for me. I hired an assistant. In fact, I've had three in the last two years. I need another one now because this one is not really getting the job done.

She is very pleasant and seems to want to help. I interviewed her carefully. We had a clear meeting in the beginning about her role and the terms of her position. But within a month, problems crept in.

The problems? For starters, she constantly waits for me to tell her what to do. She doesn't seem like the self-starter I thought I hired. Sometimes, I just wish she would do something rather than nothing.

This is a crazy market, and I am working mega-hours these days. However, she frequently wants to go home at a preset time. She's part of a big family and constantly has events with them that seem to take priority over our work here. Usually I can accommodate this, but I wish she were more flexible.

She seems to take a long time to prepare the work I give her. She wants it to be just right. I appreciate her diligence, but most of the time we can make do with a less-than-perfect document.

Perhaps worst of all, she doesn't seem to be motivated by the incentive part of her compensation. I pay her a moderate base salary but add a percentage of my personal compensation to her take-home pay. You would think this bonus opportunity would have her running around like the rest of us, trying to maximize her compensation.

I even find myself begrudging the amount that I do pay her.

THE DIAGNOSIS

Since you've been through multiple assistants and still haven't found the answer, there's clearly a mismatch in the hiring process and the reality of the job. You have continued to find people who seem to have the right combination of skills, but then somehow do not match up to your expectations.

If you summed up the experience with this assistant to date, the conclusions might look something like this:

You	The Assistant
The job is my life	The job is part of my life
Live to achieve	Live to serve
Strive to win	Strive for quality
Risk taker	Careful and steady
Make decisions quickly	Very deliberate

Your most acute pain is that she does not seem to respond to your incentive compensation structure. You know the base pay is too low without the per-deal bonus. You've assumed that she would be motivated to work as hard as you do to make the commissions from which she benefits. She likes the extra money, and she needs it, but it doesn't seem to drive her.

It's clear the two of you are wired differently.

You could hire a junior agent, and compensate him or her on full commission so you would only have a "variable cost"—paying only for performance. You doubt that would work, though. The junior agent would always chase deals, and never undertake all of the administrative tasks that the assistant covers. You suspect the team performance would go down if there were another dealmaker in the house.

Somehow, you've got to figure out how to work effectively with the person you hire as an assistant.

THE PRESCRIPTION

In order to make the assistant more effective in her role, start by viewing the position from her perspective. She sees you as powerful, fast thinking, aggressive, and competitive—and doing things she doesn't think she could ever do. She sees the two of you as completely different from each other. She believes her role is to help you be more organized, more thorough, and more compliant. She wants to help you win.

As her leader, you have to think about how you define success in her role. Consider empowering her in four ways to make her more effective:

Offer a crystal-clear understanding of the tasks for which she is responsible.

In the beginning of the relationship, take extra time to ensure she gets ample feedback from you. Show her samples of things you like and dislike. If you are already using templates, ask her to use them (and improve them, if possible). If you are not using templates, ask her to develop them, and give her comprehensive feedback about their suitability.

Convey a clear perception of your standards.

At the outset of an assignment, be sure to explain what is needed, why this assignment is important, who the stakeholders are, and what the time deadline is. As she produces work, you must give her feedback on its quality and timeliness. Show her how the work impacts the team. You may find that her standards are higher than yours. If so, discuss any compromises that will enable you to agree on quality.

Enable the ability to self-manage.

This is crucial: The assistant must be able to prioritize the assignments she is given. She must also have the ability to know how her efforts "move the needle." As an example, an effective assistant will understand that the property flyer has to be accurate because it drives the exposed information in all other marketing channels. Ideally, the assistant produces the flyer in a timely manner, submits it to the other channels, tests the output, and keeps it all on a tracking chart. When she reports at the weekly meeting that three new flyers were added to the website this week and two others were edited, you'll know she is self-managing. Often, *you* will be the source of delay or inaccuracy, and you must give her the authority to manage her processes effectively. (Decoded: you report to her on this issue!)

Give her the confidence to improve and grow.

As soon as possible, ask the assistant for her suggestions on how to improve a form or process. If she understands the process well enough to make a valuable suggestion, you know she fully understands the implications of the process. (Note to self: hire assistants who love to learn.) Eventually, ask her what she sees in your world that she could do for you. Occasionally challenge her to consider taking responsibility for a greater share of the outcomes. Using the example above, could the website designer report to her?

Here's the second piece of the puzzle: change her compensation structure. You've already acknowledged that she is wired differently than you—does it make sense to pay her like you pay yourself? My suggestion is to raise her base pay so that she is fully comfortable in her supporting role. Then meet for a formal quarterly review and award a bonus based on her contributions to the team's processes. Instead of rewarding her for the completion of the deal (that she did not generate and could not directly affect), reward her for enabling you to do more deals.

In his book *Drive: The Surprising Truth About What Motivates Us*, Dan Pink outlines the results of research showing that satisfaction with our work usually flows from factors other than compensation. According to Pink, purpose, autonomy (self-management), and mastery (growth) are more motivating than money. Further, money is only motivational if it is too low—in other words, people quit for too little money, but they do not stay because of money. They stay—and thrive—when they understand how they contribute to the team's success.

Hmm. While you've been trying to motivate the assistant with money, perhaps she was looking for something else. Take time to retool how the role works, and how it is compensated. Think about the role from the perspective of the assistant. Put your assistant in a position to help you become more powerful by empowering her.

ONE MORE THING

When I get pushback on this advice, I tell the contrasting stories of two very successful agents. The first agent is absolutely dominant in her niche. She hired a personal assistant who was paid on a commission-only basis: 10% of whatever the agent made. The assistant trailed along in the wake of the agent and was completely consumed in administrative activities. When I arrived on the scene, the compensation mechanism had caused the personal assistant to make well over $150,000 in the prior year. When I inquired what the problem was, the agent stated that the assistant didn't seem very motivated. She was also frustrated that the assistant had never generated any business that benefited the team. She assumed the assistant would respond to the additional bonus for finding new business paid in addition to the basic 10% portion.

I checked in with the assistant, who told me that she had generated two opportunities that were both refused by the agent. "She told me that we would 'ruin our brand' if we put signs on those two dogs. Now, I don't even try to get listings; I just do what I'm told."

When I closed the loop with the agent, it became clear that the mismatch was complete. The agent clearly needed an assistant but had structured the compensation for a junior producer. Even worse, the assistant (despite earning what was probably three times the compensation appropriate for the position) had a sour attitude and was chafing under the agent's expectations.

I compare this story to that of the agent with the most effective assistant I've come across. Formerly, the assistant was a teacher who left that career unfulfilled. When she started working with the agent, she used all of the valuable "teacher" skills (planning curriculum, organizing children, attending staff meetings, grading homework, posting grades and keeping the parents happy) that have a lot of application in our world. The agent realized that his assistant was a "server"—she hadn't pursued teaching for the money; she was driven to help. The agent astutely positioned her so that once he generates the deal, she moves into the control tower and lands the plane. Today, this empowered assistant is paid in admiration, praise, time off, mentoring opportunities—and the occasional bonus to supplement her healthy salary.

CHAPTER 7

WE MAKE THE SAME MISTAKES OVER AND OVER AGAIN

Prescription: Take time to carefully refine your goals and create revealing metrics

THE PAIN

The client on the phone is calling for the second time this month to inquire about the activity report on the listing she awarded six weeks ago. She is rightfully concerned about the progress you've made in marketing the property. As her voice rises, you fight the urge to make a curt reply. It's true that you promised an update twice per month, and true that you haven't issued a report yet. It sure seems easier to get the listing than to execute it!

When the call is over, you reflect on how busy you are—and yet need to become even busier. Somehow the promises you make repeatedly fall by the wayside. You start to call your partner to ask for help, but realize she's touring with a prospect all day. When the phone rings on your assistant's desk without being answered, you remember that she is dropping off a package for you.

Something has to change. Your team is busy but inefficient. Perhaps even worse, tensions have begun to seep in as the daily task list gets longer. You've even started repeating your mistakes, which drives you crazy. You've heatedly stated that "We must do a better job," which your teammates answered in silence. Your mind floats back to the call that just ended, and you grimace.

Where's my stinking report? Why can't you guys just do what you said you would do?

THE DIAGNOSIS

In some ways, it isn't surprising that your team is so busy. You have significant skills, leveraged by a strong reputation and an active market. All of the work you've done to build market share has finally paid off. How could it turn out to be so agonizing?

Your agony has two likely causes: You may not have all the skills on your team for it to do its best work, and your goals may not be aligned.

First, you may have significant skills within the group, but they may not be complementary. This often occurs when the lead team member hires additional team members that are too similar to him or herself. This is understandable—in the interview, you were both on the same page very quickly. You liked them and they liked you. They looked into your eyes and laughed at your jokes. It was an easy hire.

Unfortunately, teams where all of the partners have similar skills often have great strengths and great weaknesses. If players on the team are highly analytical, the team may be outstanding as an advisor to its clients, but it may have trouble finding clients to advise. In your case, the team has outstanding business development skills and weak processing skills. On the positive side, the friendly, persuasive, competitive nature of your team earns a lot of business. On the negative side, the dread of detail and the need for constant change causes your team to suffer when it is time to execute the business.

The second likely cause for your agony is that your goals have become fuzzy. Everyone on the team assumes that the goal is to make as much money as possible. Often, that goal is interpreted individually—each team member pursues that goal in the way they would do it as an individual.

If you took the time to change the mantra of the team to "let's make as much money as we can *as a team*," the individuals would see their role more clearly as part of a unit in which all responsibilities are shared. The daily self-talk for a team member might change from "I've got to make as many calls as I can today" to "Completing this report in an accurate and timely fashion is the most important contribution I can make to the team today."

Obviously, these two factors are related. The ideal scenario is to hone the team's goals and assemble a set of complementary skills to achieve those goals. In his well-known book *Good to Great*, Jim Collins charges leaders with these first two responsibilities: Get the right people on the bus, and get those people in the right seats on the bus.

As a first step, what is your bus? Where is it going?

> **If you took the time to change the mantra of the team to "Let's make as much money as we can *as a team*," the individuals would see their role more clearly as part of a unit in which all responsibilities are shared.**

THE PRESCRIPTION

It's time to take a serious look at your goals. Perhaps, when you started this adventure, your goal was simply "to make a lot of money." As you have progressively achieved that goal, you're realizing that your goals have to evolve. Your new goals may include delivering outstanding client service, maintaining superior market knowledge, achieving a dominant market share, and maximizing repeat business. Have these goals been thoroughly discussed with your team members? Are the expectations you hold of your team members fair to them? Have you helped them interpret these goals into their daily activities?

Arriving at a set of goals that are compelling to all team members is not an easy task. It takes time. But without convicting goals, the team can dissolve into chaos as the team members pursue whatever activities seem most logical to them.

The authors of *The 4 Disciplines of Execution* offer outstanding insight into how to formulate and track team goals. Their description of "lag" and "lead" measures related to goal achievement is particularly valuable. As an example, your team may have a goal of achieving a 20% market share. This would be the lag measure—the result that can only be evaluated at the end of the year. What is the most effective lead measure? In other words, what can you do each day that will eventually produce the desired lag-measure result? The authors offer outstanding advice on how to create accountability and tracking around your goals. If you are struggling to define goals and break them down into daily tasks, I strongly encourage you to read this book.

Here are two easy ways to tell whether your team is in sync in relation to its goals.

Is your team organizational chart meaningful to your clients and prospects?

Almost all teams have an organizational chart. Ideally, the org chart would flow from the team's goals and be a meaningful part of a marketing presentation. As an example, if you offered both landlord and tenant representation services, the org chart would show these divisions. It might also show that the divisions are supported by research and marketing specialists who serve the entire team. This org chart might be explained to the client by saying, "We have two primary focal points—landlord representation and tenant representation. One group calls primarily on tenants, while the other calls on landlords. This causes each division to be deeply knowledgeable in their niche. All of our agents are supported by research and marketing specialists who serve the entire team. This enables us to be of service to any client seeking a comprehensive understanding of the marketplace. This is the structure that has caused us to enjoy market-leading performance."

I've seen org charts that have only names (not roles) in the boxes. When I inquire what a specific person does for the team, I'll get an answer like, "He reports to me. He covers a variety of tasks. Right now, he spends most of his time on a research report I need." I've also seen org charts in which fourteen people report to one producer. These org charts essentially tell the client that you're a one-man show. They may conclude that you're the only person on the team who can help them, or that you are too busy to provide consistently high service to them.

If your org chart is merely a personnel directory, then you have given insufficient thought to how your team expresses its goals and, thus, structure. Ideally, the client would quickly understand the structure and be able to interpret it to his own benefit. When you express the goals of the structure you are showing him, he gets it. Try this experiment: Hand your existing org chart to a friend and, without any introduction, ask them to explain the structure to you. You'll find out quickly whether your team's org chart reflects your goals.

Can the team members work autonomously?

If everyone on the team understands the goals and has worked together to translate those goals into their own daily activities, they generally know what to do at any given time. During stable times, the team will operate quickly and smoothly. In more chaotic times, an individual may have to rely heavily on an understanding of the goals. It may be that a mistake is made, but if the team member can support his actions because he was pursuing the goal as he understood it, the mistake should be a learning experience and easily eliminated.

If you find that a team member constantly waits to be told what to do, or always seems to have many questions, they probably don't understand the team goals and their role in achieving those goals. Ask this question at the next team retreat: "What can we do to enable greater autonomy by each team member?"

Let's return to the idea of complementary skills among the team's members. Once we have carefully crafted goals that are understood and autonomously pursued by each team member, aren't we good to go?

Maybe. It could turn out that team members are sufficiently skilled to perform the roles that achieve the team's goals. It is just as likely, though, that the goals require activities and tasks from the team members for which they are not well-suited. In Collins-speak, you may have to move the players around on the bus to get them in the right seats. This often requires time and patience. A team member may have to sacrifice a preferred activity for one that is less natural to them. They may also have to be willing to learn a new skill.

Think back to that interview in which you were both on the same page and talked so easily. How would the interview have transpired if you discussed the team's goals and that individual's role in achieving those goals? As you ponder that interview now, do you see similar or complementary skills in the two of you?

If it seems exhausting to stop and do the work of a Collins' leader, compare that to the stress you feel every time you get a barbed comment from a disappointed client. In the long run, you can strengthen your team by scrutinizing your collective goals and skills, and intentionally matching them.

ONE MORE THING

Now that *Good to Great* has been out for 15 years, much feedback has accumulated. Business leaders who have employed Collins' message frequently say they have hired fewer people as a result of using his principles. They note that when the goals are clearly defined, a handful of the right people can get the job done. It's not uncommon to hear them say that although the Great Recession was horribly painful, it caused them to economize as the recovery ensued. Now, they get more work done now with five goal-driven, autonomous team members than the fifteen people who used to be in that department.

We're not arguing whether you're busy. You are. We're pondering whether the solution is to simply suffer through a busy season with occasional broken promises or hire more bodies to throw at the problem or become more acutely aligned with goals on the team. Leadership is hard work—but refusing to lead causes an even harder slog.

CHAPTER 8

I KNOW HE DRAGS OUR TEAM DOWN, BUT I JUST CAN'T LET HIM GO

Prescription: The wrong player in the wrong seat must be remedied

THE PAIN

You grimace as you dial Andy's number. This is the second time this week you've had to call him to discuss something that bothers you. Making these calls grinds on you, and as you wait for Andy to pick up, you wonder if it is time for a change.

You feel stuck. Andy has been with you from the beginning. His loyalty was crucial, particularly in the low part of the cycle. You have a lot of shared memories, including driving out to your first listing in his truck and installing the sign yourselves. In those days, the business seemed pretty simple—you really didn't think; you just acted on what was right in front of you.

Andy has a lot of skills. He's helped you close a lot of deals, and he's well known to your clients. However, he hasn't really evolved. It's been impossible to build a team around him, and he insists on continuing to do things as you always have. Andy acknowledges that the world has changed, but he's been stubborn about changing the practices that have succeeded in the past.

Although she didn't say it, you suspect Jessica left the team because of Andy's rigidity. Jessica loved her role on the team, and constantly offered new ideas and strategies. Perhaps she got closed down one too many times by Andy. Now, she supports one of the teams at a competing firm.

Because he was here at the beginning, Andy gets a significant share of the team's commission income. Lowering his split to reflect his reduced contribution to the team is a possibility, but not a solution. He would be deeply hurt, and if he somehow agreed, he'd be an even bigger drag on the team's morale.

It's unbearable to think about dismissing him from the team. Clients will be surprised, and competitors will crow about it. It will cause a tremendous burden on the team until you can replace him. It's possible that you will eventually take two steps forward, but this one step backward will be extremely difficult. You hear the click as Andy connects.

"Hi Andy. Do you have a few minutes to talk?"

THE DIAGNOSIS

We've all had experiences that affirm our belief that getting the wrong player off the team is a crucial function of the leader. Whether you recall a high school sports team, the crew at your summer job, or the executive committee of a large organization, you distinctly remember the impact of the wrong player.

In the beginning, your goal was simply to survive. You were desperate not to fail, and Andy joined the quest on that basis. You were both completely committed, and eventually your combined efforts got traction. Over the years, you've earned significant money and a reputation as a market leader, bolstered by a solid client base.

However, your goal has evolved from survive (not fail) to thrive (reach your full potential). The opportunity over the next decade is to leverage all of your team's assets and reach new heights of performance. In order to do that, you will have to evolve from the blunt force, mass-marketing tactics you used in the past into more customized, client-centric activities. As an example, building stronger relationships with your top clients will create much more income than making another 500 new prospect calls.

This all became clear to you as you listened to a recent industry speaker. The theme of his presentation was "Adapting to the Future in the Commercial Real Estate Industry." The basic message was that the influences of technology, particularly in the realm of communication, are so disruptive to the commercial real estate arena that we must be adaptive and flexible in these highly dynamic times. What worked in the past is not going to work in the future. The speaker went on to say there is a strong possibility that technology will diminish the need for real estate brokers.

"Adaptive and flexible" do not describe Andy. The time has come to evaluate the strategy of the team as it operates in this new environment. Part of that strategy is to arm the team with the right players. Andy may be a casualty of evolution.

THE PRESCRIPTION

In the previous chapters, we noted the first two challenges from Jim Collins: Get the right people on the bus, and get them in the right seats. Many people forget the third leg of the Collins leadership mandate—the leader must get the wrong people off the bus. According to Collins, there is no

> **A right player in the wrong seat will usually still be viewed as a valuable member of the team.**

greater destructive force to the right people than a wrong person. The right people can overcome almost any external obstacle, but a cancer from within is often fatal.

There are many warning signs that a wrong person is on the team. Most are fairly obvious—apathy, complaints, negative body language, social segregation, and refusal or denial. It occurs to you that Andy seems to work from home a lot more often. His three-page email, sent at 1:15 AM, criticizing the presentation to the Jenkins family, fried the entire team. If you're getting signals like these, your Spidey sense should be tingling. You must stop and reckon with this kind of feedback, particularly if it comes from your strongest players.

It is possible that Andy is a right player but not in the right seat. If so, you might experience frustration, resistance, and passionate argument. You'll have to take the time to discern what you're hearing and feeling. Are the arguments about how to make progress, or are they more like personal attacks? One clue is to evaluate the interpersonal relationships. A right player in the wrong seat will usually still be viewed as a valuable member of the team.

Once you've made the decision to remove a player from the team, you must act quickly and decisively. Most experienced managers say their most common mistake when firing someone was waiting too long. Every day you wait increases the danger of losing someone else on the team.

Here are the tactics I recommend as you make this move:

1. **Ensure that the team's goals and directions are clearly stated.**

    This is the guiding light. The dismissal is not personal. It is occurring because the team member no longer fits the team's strategy. Take the time to have a meeting with yourself: Can you rationally lay the capabilities of the to-be-dismissed player and the strategy for the future side-by-side, and see a distinct mismatch?

2. **Mastermind the team message in advance.**

    Before you initiate the dismissal, be sure you can clearly express the team's strategy. Practice saying it aloud. Regardless of whether you are defending the move or stating the vision for the future, the message should be the same. As an example, you might say: "We're very proud of our past accomplishments but are focused on our goals for the future. We believe we'll have to be quicker to adapt than ever before as we strive to serve the best interests of our clients. We intend to use all available resources, including technology, to remain leaders in market."

3. **Be firm.**

    Set clear guidelines for the departure. Be specific about timing. Resist the temptation to argue, criticize, or fight back. If you are challenged with legal action, simply acknowledge that option. Don't fight issues that don't exist.

4. **Be generous.**

    In 40 years of managing agents, I've never wished I was more punishing to an agent as he departed. I believe you will sleep better if you are more generous than you wanted to be. Brighter days are ahead for both of you. If the generosity enables you to complete the surgery more quickly and leave room for a future relationship, it's worth it.

    > I've never wished I was more punishing to an agent as he departed.

5. **Draw support from the remaining team members.**

    Leadership can be tough and lonely. Treat yourself to interaction with your team. They will be empathetic, and very respectful of your leadership. Their support is gratifying and necessary. Focus on the future. Okay guys, what steps can we take today that advance progress on our goals?

Evolution is inevitable. Championship teams continually hone their rosters. The most consistent champions achieve greatness by blending their year-to-year leaders with new talent and fresh approaches. If you believe that Collins' work is valid, you become great when you get the right players on the bus and the wrong ones off.

ONE MORE THING

Early in my career, I was approached by a young man I didn't know. He told me he had worked under, and had been dismissed by, my father at the Air Force Academy. The service academies take deserved pride in their team approach, and it is unusual for a team member to be removed. The dismissal led him to resign from the Air Force. Ouch.

The man went on to say that he was shocked at the time, but can now clearly see that he was the wrong player on the team. He later discovered that he was much happier in a different role in civilian life. He credits my father for helping him grow, even though the medicine was hard to swallow at the time. "Ultimately, it all turned out for the best," he said. He also stated that he had come to see that my father had exhibited supreme leadership.

THRIVE: PART THREE

RUN YOUR OPERATION AS A BUSINESS

CHAPTER 9

I HATE THIS TIME OF YEAR—I DREAD ALWAYS HAVING TO START OVER

Prescription: A business like yours demands a cash-flow projection

THE PAIN

It's the first week of December. There are three weeks left in the year, and you want to bring in as much revenue as you can, now that you've reached the highest split in your commission structure. If you can get the big land deal to close, you're golden. You have a lot to do, and a lot of distractions—all of the usual whirlwind, plus the seasonal obligations you can't escape. You've got a lot on your mind. The grind is wearing on you.

For starters, you're tired. It has been a long pull to get back in the top tier of the money list in the office. You want to get back in the Top Five so you can retake your rightful spot on the Wall of Fame in the office.

You haven't been sleeping all that great. Somewhere in the night you wondered if your luck would hold. You've calmed yourself; you've even worn your lucky socks for a week straight.

Hey, it's not the end of the world if I don't make it. I'm still going to make more money than most of the guys in the office.

You know you're rationalizing—it's been your goal all year, but goals are supposed to be a stretch, right?

It would help if the manager didn't keep asking you about it. It seems like the only time you see him is when he is "just checking in" to casually ask for the second time this week how the land deal is going. His constant poking about "the ton of Top Five competition we've got this year" just might earn him a poke in the nose.

Your brain makes the turn for another trip around the worry track.

I'm three friggin' weeks from starting over.

THE DIAGNOSIS

Your frustration is plainly evident. You're feeling all of the pain of having to manage yourself—but knowing that you're not doing a great job. You can bring in the dough—you're a proven closer and a Top Five performer—but as far as running your business, you've got some significant gaps.

For starters, you aren't generating enough of the right information to help you gain a meaningful picture of the future. You're agonizing over what you cannot see, not what you can see. You work in a very risky business—what can be more risky than 100% commission compensation?—but you aren't managing the risk very well.

The agony is compounded by your fixed—and rising—living expenses. You're not out of control, but a house payment, two leased cars, and private-school tuition keep you running hard. Your expenses are clear, but your income is vague. Fear that you might fall short one of these days translates to malaise that penetrates even your toughened intestines.

Perhaps worst of all, the constant drumbeat (internal and external) from the Wall of Fame causes you to constantly compare yourself to others. This is a bad idea. Instead of celebrating what you have accomplished, you're focused only on what you haven't gotten done. Nothing the other salespeople or manager are doing has any impact on you, but you've let "comparison" seep in to your self-talk. You've treated yourself to a pint-size cocktail with equal parts envy, arrogance, disappointment, and anxiety.

THE PRESCRIPTION

Want some relief? Make a commitment right now to a fully featured pipeline report.

I don't mean the hastily scribbled roster of deals that you turn in on scrap paper once a month to your manager; the one you submitted by voicemail last month. I'm talking about a detailed cash-flow projection for your business.

Your team has handled $45,000,000 in transaction value so far this year for twenty-three clients and grossed $2,350,000 in total commission revenue. If you ran a chain restaurant or a profit center for a national company or a doctor's office that generated these kinds of numbers, you'd have a detailed forecast that you constantly updated—or you would lose your job.

You've shortchanged yourself. Why not take a fraction of those killer skills that make you a great agent and apply them to your own business? Just like the doctor with lifesaving skills, you have to provide critical skills for your clients *and* run a practice. Does it seem logical to you that you have an MBA on your team that provides analysis to your clients, and you run your business on scrap paper?

It isn't hard to implement the fix; many detailed templates and online tools are available to you. However, you can make your own in Excel in 30 minutes. I've included a detailed example in Appendix B that you can build, if you wish. Once the form is correct, log every deal that has a chance or better of closing. Update it every week on Sunday night or Monday morning. That 15 minutes per week will change your life.

Need more convincing? Let's work backward. Imagine using a spreadsheet to answer these questions for yourself:

1. **What deals are in front of me that have a better than 75% chance of closing?**

    This usually means that both parties to the deal are identified, and documents are changing hands between them. I often see these deals color-coded as green on the spreadsheet. This enables you to focus on getting the green deals across the line on a timely basis. When the chaos is in full bloom, stay focused on the green deals.

2. **Do I have all commission payments associated with my green deals logged in?**

    In other words, who takes responsibility for invoicing and collecting the second half of that leasing commission you generated six months ago? Use the pipeline report to eliminate those sharp pains that occur when you discover that Accounting forgot to invoice the client because they thought you were doing it.

3. **What can I do today to improve my financial picture?**

    The green deals have a lot of momentum already. Take a look at the next tier of deals—those deals that are rated between 51% and 75%. What can I do today to turn these deals green?

4. **How long does the typical deal take from the day it arrives on the pipeline report until the day the commission is collected?**

    Did you realize you will have to generate the deal by June 15 to get paid this year? This means you will have to track start and stop dates for a year, and when enough deals close, you can calculate average duration. It also means you may realize you're going to fall short in November and December—but you realize it six months before it happens. Instead of worrying, you can adapt. It turns out that children can survive public school, especially if you make the transition between grades rather than at Thanksgiving.

5. **What are the primary sources of my deals?**

    This means you will have to log the source of your deals so that when they close, you can attribute dollars to sources. Brokers who track this closely know the leading sources of their revenue (prospecting, other brokers, referrals, company generated, etc.), and they nurture those sources actively.

6. **Even though I have to revert to the shallow end of the commission splits when the new calendar year begins in three weeks, when do I expect to make it to the next step on the ladder?**

    Would it be easier to stomach the lower commission splits at the start of each year if you knew that you would be on a higher tier by mid-April? A detailed cash-flow projection with a line on the spreadsheet that computes cumulative earnings year-to-date will show your exact path to the more favorable split.

7. **How does this upcoming year look in comparison to last year?**

    This means you have to save your pipeline report as a unique document each month. You need a spreadsheet saved as Dec.31.2016 and another as Dec.31.2017. You've forgotten (or never knew) that you rolled into this year with $125,000 of gross revenue identified rated at 75% probability. Now you can see that you have $187,000 of gross revenue in the same category already programmed for next year. If you don't make the Wall of Fame this year, the best medicine is to get a jump on it for next year.

Perhaps you can see now that your anxiety is your own fault. You starved yourself unnecessarily from valuable information that was at your fingertips all along. As the saying goes, you were so busy working *in* the business that you never worked *on* it. You may not like all of the information you gather, but a problem identified is a problem half solved. You can exchange your anxiety cocktail for an energy bar filled with resolve.

ONE MORE THING

I've had agents listen to this guidance and then say to me, "Tracking deals is bad luck. I'd rather just collect the money when it comes in."

Okay. You're an adult—you get to make your own choices. I would only counter that every agent I know who has made the effort to build and use a tracking system would never go back to karma and scrap paper as a recipe for financial management of their multi-million dollar business.

Just out of curiosity, how big would your business have to be before you finally decided to invoke a deal-tracking system?

CHAPTER 10

MY BROKER CARES ONLY ABOUT THE NEXT CHECK I AM SUPPOSED TO BRING IN

Prescription: Derive maximum value from your brokerage platform

THE PAIN

"Hey, Bud. How ya doing?"

Those words grate on you. You never see your broker unless he wants something from you. Now he's back at your door again. You wonder what he wants this time. Another update on your big deal? Your most recent pipeline report? A few minutes of your time to interview a potential hire?

Your relationship with the broker is only so-so. To you, he is just the "No!" man, charged with the responsibility of telling you what the company cannot do. Apparently the firm is on such a tight budget there is no chance of getting anything new approved. You generally treat him as a necessary evil. The less time you have to spend with the broker, the better.

To be fair, you realize that the broker has to supervise a lot of people, and some of them are pretty hard to manage. He has to file an unending stream of reports. He attends remote corporate meetings about a third of his time. On top of that, the firm wants him to generate commissions to offset his salary.

It would be great if the broker would give you more support. Occasionally, you force that support by asking for his feedback on a project or presentation. In your mind, you deserve that support as a top producer. Wouldn't it be great if he came to your door, just once, to give you something rather than take something?

Where are my headphones? If I put them on, I can pretend I'm too busy to talk.

THE DIAGNOSIS

You wouldn't want the broker's job, would you?

To you, it's a crummy job. There is a lot of pressure to perform and unending deskwork. You might be surprised to find that he wouldn't want your job, either. There is no underlying compensation, and you have to hustle every day.

If it is true that you are running a small business on the broker's platform, what unique advantages does the platform provide?

In addition to the different perspectives, the two of you also have different employment arrangements. Most likely, he's an employee and has a finite job description. He has a boss, he gets a bonus, and he gets two weeks of paid time off. As an independent contractor, you can work whenever you want, and you don't have to attend any meetings. You don't take "vacation"—you can take as much time away from the office as you desire.

This gulf between perspectives and work arrangements has caused you to become indifferent to management. You are associated with each other but have significantly different goals. Both of you want you to bring in a large amount of commission revenue, but your rewards from that income are different. He wants accurate forecasts and documentation and compliance. You want quick collection and relationship and opportunity. It's no surprise your relationship is only so-so.

What's been lost in translation is the value proposition. If you viewed your association with the firm as a franchise scenario, you would ask yourself: What am I getting for the revenue I pay to the firm? If it is true that you are running a small business on the broker's platform, what unique advantages does the platform provide?

THE PRESCRIPTION

In a true franchising environment, the franchisee has a crystallized understanding of what he gets from the franchisor. Think about a franchise you know. Make a list of the benefits that the franchisee receives. Your list might include marketing, procedures, hiring, best practices, materials, master vendor relationships, shipping, storage, peer relationships, group discounts, and many more.

What is it that you expect from your broker?

Your list might be simple: workspace, conference space, storage space, phone system, marketing templates, basic administrative support, marketing expertise, website management, sign construction and installation—and perhaps, a reserved parking space. These are valid expectations, but are they unique?

Think about it this way: Wherever you place your license, you have to give up some portion of your gross commission income to the brokerage platform in exchange for a package of benefits. This exchange might be called the firm's value proposition to you. (You already know that different firms offer different value propositions. For example, the residential real estate brokerage strategy of offering very few benefits for a very low split to the house is advancing in our industry.) Do you get only "industry standard" benefits for the money you pay to the platform?

Could you find a way to improve that value proposition? Could you make the platform's benefits unique instead of merely customary?

Here are six ways you can maximize the value proposition of the platform to you:

- Unless the broker will demand a piece of the action, tell the broker about your Top Ten relationships. Ask the broker to be sensitive to anything he hears about these clients/prospects and to alert you whenever he hears of something significant. In effect, the broker becomes an early warning system for you. He'll do it because he likes the idea of making a special (but low cost) contribution to one of his top producers.

- Give your broker a calling list of five prospects you have been unable to penetrate. "Hey, Bob, here are five firms that I have been trying to infiltrate without any success to date. Could you make it your business to call on them and talk about our firm?" Bob probably has some business development responsibilities and would probably appreciate some input on how to make those efforts most productive.

- Ask to direct the company's charity dollars, even if they are small. Find a way to invest those dollars in an organization or cause that accelerates your relationship with a key prospect or influencer. Buy a table at the gala sponsored by the client. Buy a team in the charity golf event, and invite the CEO to play with you. Even if the invitation is declined, you score points with the prospect.

- Ask to direct the company's trade association dollars, or at least act as the company's representative at the monthly meetings. It isn't unusual to receive the right to make a presentation or accept an award when a brokerage firm supports a trade association. These opportunities may enlarge your visibility in the arena.

- Ask to be consulted whenever the company is approached by a media outlet to provide a statement or reaction. The broker may handle these requests himself, or he may be pleased to have some relief. Make sure you have a current media-ready photograph and bio available for quick release.

- Invite the broker to attend a presentation with you. Explain that you aren't asking him to have a speaking part; instead, you want to demonstrate the firm's support of your efforts. He may get the chance to add a brief affirmation of your outstanding client service capabilities. Many prospects like to know that they have the attention of the leader. This can be especially important when you are competing against larger firms. Ask the broker to take notes during the presentation, and discuss his feedback afterward.

Hopefully, this list has spurred ideas about other ways your broker can become more valuable to you. The next time you're tempted to investigate changing firms, take a moment to think through how you can make this platform, the one in which you are already powerful, more valuable than a competing platform.

Ultimately, why leave this relationship as one of indifference? Whatever split you pay to the house is too much for merely lukewarm support. Strive to get more than the customary benefits. Be the guy of whom it is said, "Nobody leverages the house better than he does!"

ONE MORE THING

Most managing brokers have their hands full. They are very busy and often forced to deal with squeaky wheels, if only for their own sanity.

I offer this advice as a former manager who once had responsibility for thirty producers. I wanted to propel my agents with coaching and support, but I was almost always in Quadrant I (urgent and important). I rarely had the opportunity to play offense—to go to an agent and say, "How can I help you?"

You may work with a broker who is truly indifferent, and you might have to contemplate a change. If you decide to consider a change, I strongly urge you to think in terms of "value proposition" instead of only a more favorable commission split. If the weighted average commission split to you at the new firm is more than 70%, you are highly likely to lose benefits. Or, as the new broker would say, "If you need that benefit, you'll have to pay for it yourself." Make sure you carefully consider the entire value proposition and the net commission dollars you will receive after you get the benefits you need.

(A word to managing brokers: Luring a competitive agent to your firm with a hugely favorable split to the agent is probably a losing proposition. When a managing broker tells me they had to pay the big split to win and they view it as a loss leader, I know storm clouds are on the horizon. The arrival of the new top gun does not automatically mean that the rest of the staff will suddenly start covering their desk costs. Ultimately, having the firm fail around the top gun is troublesome for everyone involved.)

For me, I always wanted to use Tom Cruise's line as a frustrated sports agent in the movie, *Jerry Maguire*: "Help me help you." If your broker is open to it, help him enhance the value of the brokerage platform to your team. Leverage the platform by getting the most for the money you spend to be part of the franchise.

CONCLUSION

"I'll take him out," Rick said to his wife. "C'mon, dog, let's go tour the estate."

Rick tumbled outside with Bear, and while the dog sniffed all the usual spots, Rick recorded a few quick thoughts in his phone. When he returned to his office inside the house, Rick converted his thoughts into emails and sent them off to his teammates. They were used to his Sunday night notes. He knew they would read them almost immediately, and that the team would be prepared to discuss them at the standing team meeting in the morning.

Not surprisingly, the responses were already pinging his phone on Monday morning when Rick rose at 5:45 AM to exercise. He wasn't crazy about spinning at 6:30 AM, but it worked as a time he could spend together with his wife, and the coffee afterward on the ride home was heavenly.

When the Uber arrived at 7:30 AM, Rick was ready. He had printed a couple of the email responses so he could study the details on the ride in. He walked into the office a few minutes before 8:00 AM, and the team was already seated around the small conference table when Rick greeted them.

Rick's assistant, Jessica, went first. "Well, the most positive thing that happened to me over the weekend was watching my nephew enjoy his birthday party." Brief chatter ensued, and each team member used the allotted two minutes to give his or her "best thing" update.

The team looked to Rick. He pointed to his chief of staff. "Okay, Jon, you're up. Lead us through the reports."

Jon offered each person a three-ring binder, and said, "Let's skip over Tab 1 for the moment, and look at Tab 2. Since our last meeting, our inventory of vacant space experienced a 28,000 square foot increase—but for the right reasons. We completed two deals totaling 16,000 square feet, but we took on the vacant, 44,000-square-foot Synergy headquarters building as a new listing."

Jon proceeded to lead the team through the newly prepared reports in the other sections of the notebook. Then he invited everyone up to the whiteboard to view the latest iteration of the Gantt chart related to their biggest assignment—the $16,000,000 investment sale of an office building they had leased for the owner. The team discussed the status of several items, and Jon agreed to make the edits today before presenting it to the owner tomorrow. Overall, Rick was pleased—the team was executing on its assignments.

At 8:45 AM, Manny joined the meeting. Manny was Jorge Espinosa, a former salesperson who had accepted the role of office manager. The agents had nicknamed him "Manny" as a play on his "manager" title. Rick had asked Manny to join the meeting as soon as he was available.

"Hi, Manny. Thanks for stopping in," Rick said.

"Are you kidding?" Manny replied. "This is the best meeting of my week."

Jon directed everyone back to Tab 1. "Let's look at the pipeline report. Based on your input over the past 72 hours, I've updated the report. Since last week, we upgraded about $125,000 from yellow to green, so we had a great week in terms of advancing our deals toward closing. Two items need attention. First, Rick, we need you to call the seller's attorney on the Jenkins property. Everyone is wrapped around the axle on the timing of the permits. I'll give you more details after the meeting. The bottom line is that the deal is still rated at only 50%

probability but is supposedly only nine weeks from closing. Realistically, it should be rated higher if that is true."

Jon explained the other issue, and then said, "So, in summary, we are slightly ahead of our beginning-of-year projection—which was a projection about 15% greater than last year. In fact, we've collected about $210,000 more this year to date than at the same time last year. Best of all, I currently estimate our rollover income for next year to be 30% greater than at this time last year."

Manny loved it. "I wish I could get this clear, concise reporting from everyone. Before I check out, is there anything you need from me?" Rick smiled, and said, "Just have the checkbook ready for some massive raffle ticket purchases at the golf tournament on Friday." Manny offered double thumbs up, winked, and walked out.

It was 9:00 AM—time to adjourn. Jon collected the binders and the Gantt chart. He filled Rick in on the Jenkins attorney issue. Jessica followed Rick to his desk. "Here is the list of calls you need to make this week. Do you have last week's call notes?" Rick turned his notes over to her, which contained the details of each call attempt, and a callback date to be entered into each record. Jessica asked a few questions and said she would have all of the notes entered by the end of the day. She then showed Rick her task list for the week. They agreed on a few tweaks and reordered some priorities.

Rick spent the next two hours making calls at his desk. He put his cell phone on "Do Not Disturb." He called up the CRM record for each call and spent a minute reviewing past notes before clicking the dial button. He'd discovered that late Monday morning worked for many of his prospects, and if not, he got his voicemail logged on to their phone early in the week. This was prime time, and Rick forced himself to stay focused. At 11:15 AM, he called the attorney Jon mentioned in the earlier meeting and asked for a time to come to her office and meet in person in regard to the permits.

At 11:45 AM, Brant appeared at Rick's desk. "Time to go, Rick." Rick liked Brant, and noted that the kid had cleaned up nicely for this event. Brant was a summer intern who had been given some specific research tasks related to tenant movement in the market. As they walked the six blocks to the trade association luncheon, Rick asked about Brant's recent findings. "What trend did you identify since last week?" Brant filled Rick in, and asked for ten minutes after lunch to show him a map he was working on.

Rick lingered a few minutes after the luncheon, talking to some of his fellow agents. He didn't see his former teammate, Benton, but heard that he had decided to take some time off. Rick sent a text to Jessica: Remind me to call Benton in a month.

He asked Brant to walk with him to another building nearby. "Take a picture of the tenant directory. Compare your notes to our records in the CRM. I think the tenants in this building are in for some changes, and I would like to create a special outreach for them."

When they got back to the office, Rick looked at the map Brant had prepared and gave him some instructions for the new prospect names they had just captured. Rick checked his phone—five voicemails and twelve emails since leaving for lunch. Because he had purposefully left the after-lunch slot unscheduled, he spent the next two hours resolving all of the messages.

At 4:00 PM, Rick met with Jessica for 45 minutes to discuss the client dinner that was scheduled in two weeks. This was the third annual dinner, and they had launched some significant upgrades this year. Jessica seemed to have it all under control. "The smartest thing we did, Rick, was hire the event coordinator your wife recommended. She's an assassin on details."

Jon arrived next. It was time to review tomorrow's presentation. Jon had done a good job with the edits on the Gantt chart and even added a few new touches that Rick approved. "Okay, I'm ready. Fire away!" said

Jon. Rick smiled—Jon now knew that the preparation for a presentation always included a push/pull role play. First, Rick played the client and asked Jon to be clearer on a couple of points, and then objected to the commission rate. Then they reversed roles, and Jon played the client. "So, Rick, in no more than five words, what is the primary reason I should choose your team for this assignment?" Jon was relishing his role and playfully goading his mentor.

Rick started to call for an Uber to take him home, but one of the agents housed near Rick's cube asked if he could give Rick a ride home. "I'm going to my son's high school soccer practice and it's located about a mile from your house. Could I pick your brain?" Rick agreed, even though he had been looking forward to scrutinizing a flyer on a building he thought might work for his own portfolio. The agent wanted some guidance, since he was confidentially thinking about leaving the firm, and Rick offered his perspective. "Thanks, man, I really appreciate your input."

After dinner, Rick found himself out on the lawn with Bear again. He chatted with a neighbor and then narrated a quick email to himself on his phone. Tomorrow was going to be a great day.

APPENDIX

APPENDIX A:

A WORD TO MANAGING BROKERS (OR OWNERS) OF A COMMERCIAL REAL ESTATE BROKERAGE

The majority of brokerage managers in the country also have production responsibilities. Chances are, some of the prescriptions in this book fit your personal situation. If so, your empathy and experience will be particularly valuable to your agents as you counsel them. You may find this book will open channels of discussion as you consider the applicability of these ideas together.

Beyond empathy, though, I believe there are three mandates for your role:

Regular, periodic communication is a must.

The primary point of this book is that agents should see themselves as running a durable, sustainable business on your platform. Even as the agents progressively grasp and implement this idea, they will still need perspective and guidance. These small businesses usually operate without a board of directors, or even shareholders. You are perfectly positioned to fill all or a part of this role. If you are part of a larger organization, you get this input from your regional and national meetings, or perhaps from a peer advisory group like Vistage. You can sense how valuable it would be for an agent to have a sounding board or a provocateur or an accountability partner, or all three.

You may find that you can come alongside your salespeople with a reading plan. Most of the brokers I coach are prolific readers. They constantly ask me for recommendations. (See Appendix C for my suggested reading list.) This can be an easy way to consider new ideas and create the opportunity for periodic communication. ("Great—I look forward to it. Let's agree that we'll discuss the first four chapters at our breakfast next Tuesday.") These meetings offer that ideal chance to simply inquire about how it's going in general.

At the least, buy the salesperson a one-on-one meal occasionally. There is something about breaking bread that creates a more harmonious, more vulnerable environment for communication. Perhaps the chewing and swallowing slows down the pace of the conversation and allows more time for consideration and reflection. If I were your coach, I'd ask you to pull out your calendar and craft a record of meals you've held with each agent over the past year, all the way down to the interns. How would your record look?

Start with a pipeline report.

If you could implement only one idea to help an agent, what would it be? Based on all of my experience, I would choose the pipeline report. The single most important measure of brokerage health is the pipeline report. It focuses the agent on the most important activities, projects the agent's cash flow, reveals the source and duration of deals, serves as the return on investment for prospecting, and, when rolled up with the other agents, enables you to project the performance of your entire agency.

It's already clear to you that the pipeline report is crucial, which is why you've relentlessly pursued the agents to turn it in each month. You've probably considered adding "regular submission of an approved pipeline report on a periodic basis" to your independent contractor agreement.

The agents get it—it is valuable to you and you want it. Have you made it valuable to them?

You know from Chapter 9 that I believe it's imperative for the agent to create and use a pipeline report for the many reasons I've outlined. As important as it is to you, I believe it's an imperative for them. So, have you changed your approach from stick to carrot? You could—persuasive logic is on your side.

Recognize accomplishment whenever possible.

When I managed an office of thirty salespeople for a national company, I had the chance to visit with the CEO. As I explained how it was going and what challenges I was facing, he waited and then said, "In the end, Blaine, it boils down to this: Every agent is either a money guy or a fame guy. Some agents just want to maximize the money they draw from the business. They are indifferent to awards and notoriety. Other guys want to win every contest for the adulation it brings. Money is only the currency of their drive to be famous. Figure out which camp the guy is in, and manage him accordingly."

Many times I've pondered that remark made to me over 30 years ago. I have often seen situations when that analysis rings exactly true. Here's what I think it means to you: Fame rarely hurts and it almost always helps. If you make a big deal out of a win, large or small, the money guys may be indifferent, but they are not offended. On the other hand, the fame guys soak it in and convert it to pure adrenaline. They're totally pumped. But if you fail to shower recognition on a fame guy, he'll eventually perceive it as a slight. That slight grows into indifference and then a crevasse.

It's a competitive world out there—you've got to hang on to your productive agents. They are going to be wooed by competitors. You'll have to have a strong value proposition as a platform to keep them. But—the greatest factor in your favor is the relationship "glue" between you and your agent. If you've made regular deposits, no one can match the emotional bank account you've accumulated. It is an easy investment to take a minute to recognize the agent, whether it is a trophy, a gift, a meal, an advertisement, or just a phone call.

So, here's my special guidance for you, the manager: regular communication, value-infused pipeline reporting, and recognition whenever possible. You will still face many challenges—that's what management is—but you can contribute significantly to the performance of your agents. As you guide them to success as "franchisees" on your platform, the success of the franchise is assured.

APPENDIX B

A DETAILED PIPELINE SYSTEM

I offered my rationale for a deal-tracking pipeline in Chapter 9. I believe a durable business operation needs a cash-flow projection to sustain itself. Many additional insights can flow from careful tracking as well, and these are also detailed in the earlier chapter.

You have the option of using an existing template. Many are available online. There are also cloud-based pipeline reports that enable you to access them from your smart device and store your data online; I have several clients using PipeDrive, as an example. Many of the fully featured CRMs (e.g., SalesForce and Infusionsoft) have built-in pipeline reports, which can be somewhat customized for your use.

The purpose of this Appendix is to offer a step-by-step guide to building your own in Microsoft Excel. I have worked with Val Despard of Despard Analytics to build one from scratch so that I would be able to describe it to you. The instructions are detailed on the next page.

Want a copy of this pipeline report? Val will send you a color-coded, fully featured Excel file that you can manipulate to fit your own needs. Send Val an email at val.despard@despardanalytics.com; tell him that you read this book and would like a copy of the file. You can discuss modifications with him, too, if you will let him briefly explain the outsourced, expert commercial real estate investment modeling services that he provides.

Building a pipeline report from scratch in Microsoft Excel

- Task 1: Add a column for the name or client that identifies the deal. Some agents create two columns and name each party to the transaction. You may have to use Party 1, Party 2, etc., and identify them as buyer, seller, etc., in another column.

- Task 2: Add the remaining columns: Opportunity, Status, Price, Commission %, Total Fee, the proportion paid to you (% To Me), My Fee, Date On (the day the deal was first entered onto the spreadsheet by you), the expected Closing Date, and Probability. These fields will change as the deal evolves.

- Task 3: For the Probability column, decide on the activities that raise the probability level. Some agents add a deal to the pipeline at an entry level probability of, say, 40%, and then raise the probability as specific terms become more clear: when an LOI is generated, when a contract is signed, when the deposit becomes non-refundable, etc.

- Task 4: Color-code each row in the spreadsheet by probability. Every deal at 50% probability or less is ORANGE. The deals between 51% and 75% are YELLOW. The deals at 76%+ probability are GREEN. Then sort the spreadsheet by descending probability; all the green deals will be on top, followed by the yellow deals, followed by the orange deals. As I mentioned in Chapter 9, I tend to focus on the yellow deals—they often need the most attention when they are in the "not quite fully cooked" status.

- Task 5: Using the Date On and Closing Date columns, consider installing another column entitled Duration. Make the Duration cells equal to the time between the Date On and Closing Date.

ACTIVE DEALS

Client	Opportunity	Status	Sale/Lease Price	Comm %	Fee	% To Me	My Fee	Date On	Closing Date	Probability
Jenkins Family	Sale	Awaiting Payment	$1,750,000	3.00%	$52,500	50%	$26,250	2/28/2016	1/15/2017	95%
Japan Sushi	Lease	Awaiting Payment	$134,560	6.00%	$8,074	50%	$4,037	9/30/2016	2/28/2017	95%
Generation One	Renewal	Excl. Rep / Listing Agrmt.	$125,000	3.00%	$3,750	50%	$1,875	3/31/2017	8/31/2017	90%
Dr Vanson Clinic	Lease	Marketing / Negotiations	$600,000	3.50%	$21,000	50%	$10,500	7/31/2016	8/31/2017	85%
Attorney Ed Flanders	Lease	Excl. Rep / Listing Agrmt.	$45,777	3.00%	$884	50%	$442	7/31/2016	12/31/2016	75%
Leukemia Society	Renewal	Marketing / Negotiations	$120,836	3.00%	$3,625	50%	$1,813	10/31/2016	4/15/2017	75%
Barnhart Automotive	Lease	Marketing / Negotiations	$400,000	2.50%	$10,000	50%	$5,000	7/31/2017	8/31/2017	75%
Golf Gods Retail Storage	Lease	Excl. Rep / Listing Agrmt.	$282,000	3.00%	$8,460	50%	$4,230	3/31/2016	9/1/2017	75%
No Pain No Gain	Lease	Marketing / Negotiations	$225,343	4.00%	$9,014	50%	$4,507	9/30/2016	1/19/2017	75%
Techster	Lease	Marketing / Negotiations	$616,000	3.00%	$18,480	50%	$9,240	8/31/2016	3/15/2017	70%
Nocatee Public Works	Renewal	Excl. Rep / Listing Agrmt.	$88,000	2.50%	$2,200	55%	$1,210	1/1/2018	3/31/2018	70%
Orange Blossom Dental	Renewal	Marketing / Negotiations	$237,000	3.00%	$7,110	50%	$3,555	9/30/2016	4/1/2017	70%
Iceland Air Storage	Lease	Excl. Rep / Listing Agrmt.	$345,000	2.50%	$8,625	20%	$1,725	11/30/2017	3/31/2018	65%
Keyboarder Co	Sale	Marketing / Negotiations	$800,000	2.00%	$16,000	33%	$5,280	5/31/2016	3/16/2017	60%
Pathways Logistics	Lease	Excl. Rep / Listing Agrmt.	$302,000	2.50%	$7,550	55%	$4,153	11/30/2017	3/31/2018	55%
Surgery Society	Lease	Qualified Prospect	$176,000	6.00%	$10,560	50%	$5,280	8/31/2017	4/2/2017	50%
Kennedy Group	Lease	Qualified Prospect	$500,000	3.00%	$15,000	50%	$7,500	11/30/2016	5/31/2018	45%
Daniels Roofing	Leae	Qualified Prospect	$350,000	3.00%	$10,500	50%	$5,250	4/30/2017	5/31/2018	40%
BiPod Mechanics	Sale	Qualified Prospect	$675,000	2.50%	$16,875	40%	$6,750	6/30/2017	2/28/2018	35%
Force 1 Security	Lease	Qualified Prospect	$90,000	3.00%	$2,700	50%	$1,350	10/31/2016	4/30/2018	25%
Lakoosa Ranch	Land Sale	Qualified Prospect	$650,000	2.50%	$16,250	50%	$8,125	10/31/2016	4/30/2018	25%
Darlene Investments	Lease	Qualified Prospect	$458,000	2.75%	$12,595	33%	$4,156	5/31/2017	4/30/2018	25%
Hunter Gutters Storage	Lease	Excl. Rep / Listing Agrmt.	$225,000	2.50%	$5,625	50%	$2,813	3/1/2018	5/31/2018	15%
Family Affair Medical	Lease	Qualified Prospect	$150,000	3.00%	$4,500	50%	$2,250	10/31/2016	4/5/2017	5%
24			$9,345,516	3.11%	$271,876	47%	$127,290			58%

Appendix B | 89

(Excel can make this calculation for you if you use the proper date format.) At the bottom of this column, calculate the average duration. You can further sort this by deal type. As an example, you may find that you complete the average tenant rep transaction within six months of adding it to the pipeline report, while a land sale takes an average of 14 months to complete.

- Task 6: Consider adding a column called Source and confine it to, say, six possible sources (cold call, referral, company generated, repeat business, etc.). After you have closed several deals, you can use a pivot table to match the source with the amount of commissions (or number of deals, or both) with the source.

Over time, your deals should matriculate through the spreadsheet, moving upward from orange to yellow to green. When they are fully completed and paid, cut the individual row off this tab of the spreadsheet and paste it on to a second tab entitled "Completed Deals." This will enable you to see what you have already completed, and draw conclusions about how your business generates revenue.

If a deal dies while on the pipeline report, cut that row off this tab and paste it onto a separate tab entitled "Dead Deals." This will enable you to scrutinize the deals that have failed to close after you logged them onto the pipeline. As you look at the group of dead deals, are any trends identifiable? Are there any lessons to be learned?

I encourage agents to update their pipeline report every week. As you update the details of each transaction, you will be building a continually evolving cash flow projection. As you become more sophisticated in your use of the report, you can install advanced tools (pivot tables, graphs, and historical comparisons) to gain even more insight into your business.

APPENDIX C

BOOKS THAT HAVE BEEN MEANINGFUL TO ME

I once visited a professor's home and we ended up in a floor-to-ceiling library that had a sliding ladder to reach the top shelves. I was astounded. "Wow! You own a *lot* of books!" I said.

He responded, "I *have* a lot of books." He pointed to one shelf at chest height. "But the ones that I *own* all fit on this shelf." When I looked puzzled, he continued, "There are a lot of books in this room. I've read them all. I've enjoyed most of them. But on this shelf, I keep the books I *own*. What do I mean by 'own'? I mean that I can look just at the spine and tell you the complete message of the book. So I own *these* books—meaning that I own the message of the author, regardless of whether the book is in my possession or not."

Here are some books I own and recommend to you. The first two books listed are mentioned earlier in this book and have been particularly valuable to me:

The Seven Habits of Highly Effective People: Powerful Lessons in Personal Change
By Stephen R. Covey / Publisher: Simon & Schuster
I first attended a Covey seminar 35 years ago, and I have integrated so many components of his message into my life that they seem like a

natural reaction now. I'm disappointed in myself when I violate one of the principles. If you are going to read only one book, this is it.

The 4 Disciplines of Execution
By Sean Covey et al. / Publisher: Free Press

Because of its influence on me, I've mentioned this book throughout the text. It presents a simple plan for defining goals and breaking the pursuit of those goals into lead measures and lag measures. Your entire team will benefit from reading this.

The E-Myth Revisited: Why Most Small Businesses Don't Work and What to Do about It
By Michael E. Gerber / Publisher: HarperCollins

I haven't received my royalty check yet, but I've sold many copies of this book—since I require my consulting clients to read it before we work together. This is the gospel of process thinking: your job as a business leader is to create replicable processes that enable others to do what you once did.

The Black Swan: The Impact of the Highly Improbable
By Nassim Nicholas Taleb / Publisher: Random House

Oh, how I wish I had read this book in business school—which is why I require it of all the students I teach now. We don't know what we don't know, so we completely misjudge risk. After you read this book, you will be permanently warped (like learning that Santa Claus is not real), but also a more effective risk taker.

Traction: Get a Grip on Your Business
Get a Grip: An Entrepreneurial Fable—Your Journey to Get Real, Get Simple, and Get Results
By Gino Wickman / Publisher: BenBella Books

Here's the gospel of accountability for entrepreneurs. *Traction* is the text book, while *Get a Grip* is the same message in "business fable" format (my preference). If you want to have more effective team meetings and advance on your goals more intentionally, absorb this message.

Mr. Schmooze: The Art and Science of Selling through Relationships
By Richard Abraham / Publisher: Wiley

A quick read that conveys really just one idea—find a way to be memorable to your prospects and clients. This would be a great starter book for a team discussion or group reading plan, particularly if you intend to adopt the top-of-mind strategy explained in Chapter 1. The author publishes a brief, periodic "thought for the day" email that I enjoy, too.

Good to Great: Why Some Companies Make the Leap . . . And Others Don't
By Jim Collins / Publisher: HarperBusiness

When this book came out fifteen years ago, it was required reading in the business world. Today, the primary principles still hold true for building an effective team: Get the right people on the bus, get them in the right seats, and get the wrong people off the bus.

Thinking, Fast and Slow
By Daniel Kahneman / Publisher: Farrar, Straus and Giroux

This is the summary of Kahneman's lifelong work (for which he won a Nobel Prize). It turns out that we are not rational decision makers; we're quite emotional. It's long, but worthy of plowing through. I also found the story of Kahneman's relationship with his research partner, Amos Tversky, as told by Michael Lewis in his book, *The Undoing Project*, to be fascinating.

Drive: The Surprising Truth about What Motivates Us
By Daniel H. Pink / Publisher: Riverhead Books

Pink's exploration of motivation is valuable to team builders. It caused me to reevaluate how members of a team work together most effectively, and how leaders can weave together players who have different motivations.

Getting Naked: A Business Fable about Shedding the Three Fears That Sabotage Client Loyalty
By Patrick Lencioni / Publisher: Jossey Bass

Since reading this book, I've used Lencioni's recommended style—employing an assumptive, proprietary approach to advising clients (jump right in, and start saying "we" as soon as possible). I recommend it to anyone seeking to become a trusted advisor. Actually, I recommend all of Lencioni's work.

The Coaching Habit: Say Less, Ask More & Change the Way You Lead Forever
By Michael Bungay Stanier / Publisher: Box of Crayons Press

The subtitle says it all. If you have ever said, "I can do this myself in the same amount of time I can explain it to you," you need this message urgently.

The Back of the Napkin: Solving Problems and Selling Ideas with Pictures
By Dan Roam / Publisher: Portfolio Hardcover

If you and I work together in a coaching relationship, we'll use Post-it Note easel pads and big markers when we convene. Dan Roam contends that reducing concepts and challenges to stick-figure drawings forces you to get to the heart of the matter. It isn't a matter of artistry; it is a matter of simplicity. Try it!

Crucial Conversations: Tools for Talking When Stakes Are High
By Joseph Grenny / Publisher: McGraw Hill Education

A director of human resources at a Fortune 200 company recommended this book to me with the warning that "this is prime, prime material, but it is hard to implement and harder to master. You've got to practice constantly." I bought the book and the DVD coaching materials. If you are going to negotiate with team members, family members, and clients, you will benefit from this perspective.

I've read all of these books in print. I've also listened to many of them as audiobooks. Many have synopses available—just search the options on Amazon. Every one of these authors has multiple videos on YouTube. If you are willing to learn, many formats are available to you. If you find a favorite or two, most of the authors also have blogs or newsletters or sequels or Facebook pages or seminars, or all of these tools.

ACKNOWLEDGMENTS

Any first-time author is dependent on many people to complete the project, and I am so thankful for my many supporters.

My first thought goes to my father, Robert K. Strickland. He's a graduate of West Point, an Air Force fighter pilot, a Vietnam War veteran – and an emeritus designee of the CCIM Institute. He's a coach, an educator and a dealmaker. I entered the commercial real estate business because he did. Dad has been a continual inspiration to me throughout my career.

Wally Bock provided quick, cogent insight every time I called on him. His guidance enabled me to get on track and finish the race. I worked closely with Lindsay Warden to create story pictures of my prescriptions, and that exercise clarified my thinking many times. Lynette Smith cleaned up the draft and knocked out many errors.

John Crossman and Justin Spizman offered guidance from their own journeys as authors. Jim Spaeth, Tom Strickland (my brother), Hunter Strickland (my son) and Casey Strickland (my daughter) all read various versions of the manuscript. They gave me feedback, corrected errors and pushed me along in the process.

In addition to writing the Foreword, Rod Santomassimo continually responded to my questions and helped me navigate the process at every turn. There wouldn't be a book without Rod.

Finally, my partner of more than 37 years, my wife, Eileen, was a constant encourager, reader, listener and muse. She supports me in so many ways that she deserves the most credit of all.

ABOUT THE AUTHOR

H. Blaine Strickland has been in the commercial real estate business since he was twenty years old. He transferred to the University of Florida in 1977 as a junior so he could major in real estate. (UF was one of the few schools that had a full slate of real estate professors and a formal undergraduate and graduate degree program at that time.) By the end of his junior year, he had a Florida real estate salesperson license and a summer job with an appraiser in Tampa. By the time he left UF, he had a graduate degree, a broker's license (which has been active ever since), and a year's worth of work experience with the appraiser. He had even closed a few deals on his own!

A couple of years later, Blaine became one of the first salespeople hired by Coldwell Banker (the company now known as CBRE) when it opened in Tampa. He had quick success there and eventually became one of the youngest profit center managers ever. The lessons learned in the job of "resident manager" for Coldwell Banker are the seeds of the prescriptions offered in this book.

After ten years with Coldwell Banker, Blaine spent the next two decades with various firms as he learned how to become a developer and owner of commercial real estate. He was fortunate to work on some very large projects, and then, when he started his own firm, some comparatively small ones. Along the way, he learned how to start companies and finish projects effectively. He knows what it's like to stretch to make payroll, negotiate with municipalities, fire contractors, raise millions of dollars, and sign personally on very large loans.

Finally, as Blaine started his fourth decade in the business, it was time to bundle all of his experiences and skills by formally calling himself a coach. He had been teaching classes at UF, UNC-Chapel Hill, the University of Central Florida, and at the CCIM Institute for several years. He enjoyed the teacher's role of learning and sharing, and still does, but teaching is only a sideline for him. He wanted to work with real bullets—be on the front line with producing agents and brokerages—and he's deeply grateful to the many agents that have allowed him to come alongside them as coach, mentor, and consultant.

The messages in this book flow from all of the experiences Blaine has had in the commercial real estate industry. He's enjoyed success and endured failure. Through it all, he's continuously sought to get smarter about the business. He has a plaque in his office that contains a quote supposedly spoken by Michelangelo when he was 80 years old: *Ancora Imparo.*

"I am still learning."

Blaine Strickland is not 80 (yet), but he feels the same way. His hope is that this book will add to your understanding and extend your learning.